BIG BOOK OF
OPTICAL
ILLUSIONS

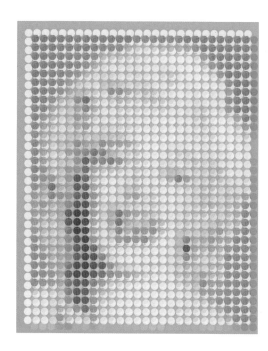

First edition for the United States and Canada published in 2006 by Barron's Educational Series, Inc.

First published in Great Britain in 2005 by Carlton Books Limited, 20 Mortimer Street, London W1T 3JW, Great Britain

American edition Copyright © 2006 by Barron's Educational Series, Inc.
Text and artwork Copyright © 2005 by Archimedes' Laboratory Ltd.
Copyright © 2005 by Carlton Books Ltd.

All inquiries should be addressed to:
Barron's Educational Series, Inc.
250 Wireless Boulevard
Hauppauge, New York 11788
http://www.barronseduc.com

ISBN-13 (Barron's): 978-0-7641-3520-0
ISBN-10 (Barron's): 0-7641-3520-1

Library of Congress Catalog Card No. 2005934856

Printed in Dubai

9 8 7 6 5 4 3 2 1

DEDICATION
For Antoinette Troïsi, my mother… who sometimes gives me the ILLUSION that the entire solar system rotates around me!
– G. Sarcone

(Page 1) Can you guess what it is?
The image is only composed of yellow, gray, and green dots, but if you look at it from a certain distance, the lovely face of Marilyn Monroe will appear, and the color of the complexion gets a flesh-colored tint… even though there's no red or orange in the picture!

(Page 3) Which color are the squares in the background?
The squares in the background could have two colors. Their color depends primarily on how we interpret the foreground objects: as a tilted series of multicolored squares, or as a grid?

BIG BOOK OF OPTICAL ILLUSIONS

Over 200 Original Deceptive Artworks & Brain-Fooling Images

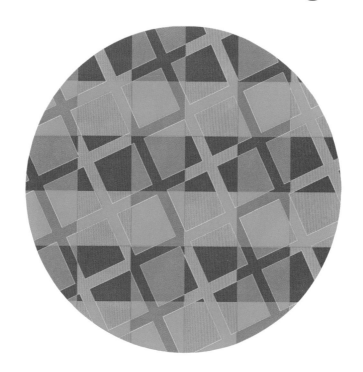

Gianni A. Sarcone & Marie-Jo Waeber

BARRON'S

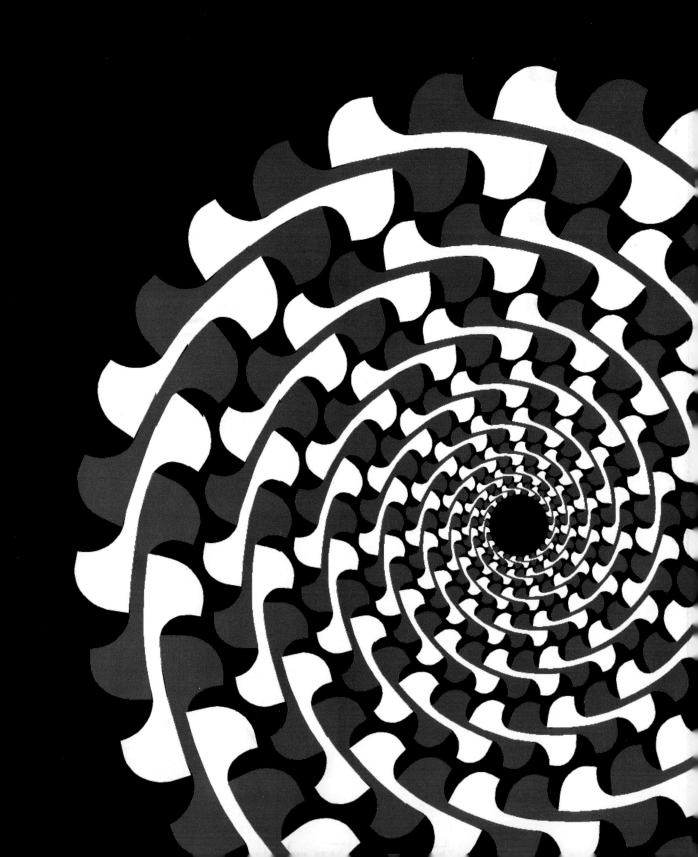

Contents

Introduction 6
Gallery I 22
  Gallery I Notes 44
Gallery II 46
  Gallery II Notes 68
Gallery III 70
  Gallery III Notes 92
Gallery IV 94
  Gallery IV Notes 116
Gallery V 118
  Gallery V Notes 140
Gallery VI 142
  Gallery VI Notes 160
Gallery VII 162
  Gallery VII Notes 184
Gallery VIII 186
  Gallery VIII Notes 208
Gallery IX 210
  Gallery IX Notes 232
Gallery X 234
  Gallery X Notes 256
Gallery XI 258
  Gallery XI Notes 268
Glossary 270
Picture Credits 272

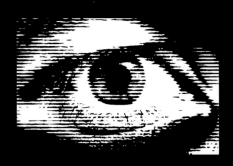

'The organizational mechanisms of
vision are best demonstrated by
illusions. Illusions illustrate that
perception is a creative construction
that the brain makes in interpreting
visual data... Learning does not
prevent us from being taken in
by these illusions'

– Eric Kandel, *Principles of Neural Science.*

INTRODUCTION

What you see isn't always what you get!

'The universe is full of magical things, patiently waiting for our wits to grow sharper,' said Eden Phillpotts. Two of these magical things are so close to our nose we often just take them for granted – we call them "eyes." Yes, we take vision for granted; that's why optical illusions are important, because they reveal the magic and the limits of our visual perception.

In the word "illusion" we find the Latin root *ludus*, which means "play." As illusions really play with our senses, they capture our attention and strike us as strange and interesting. So could it be that we are fascinated by optical illusions because we like to be mystified?

Growing literature on illusions reflects this popular interest and points to the fact that these sensations are not only interesting in themselves, but are also sources for gaining insight into normal vision. Vision isn't quite a 100 percent natural process as some people may think. It depends to a large extent on learned skills that are helpful in interpreting the real world, but can sometimes be deceiving. People in the most remote and isolated parts of the world, who have never seen photographs, cannot at first understand what a photograph depicts when it is shown to them. The interpretation of this particular kind of visual representation is a learned skill.

So what are optical or visual illusions exactly? In the fewest words, they are particular illusions that deceive the human visual system into perceiving something that is not present, or incorrectly perceiving what is present. There

are two kinds of optical illusions: physiological illusions and cognitive illusions. Physiological illusions are the effects on the eyes or brain of prolonged stimulation of a specific type: brightness, tilt, color, movement. Cognitive illusions interact with different levels of perceptual processing, and built-in assumptions or "knowledge" are misdirected. Cognitive illusions are commonly divided into ambiguous illusions, distorting illusions, paradox illusions, or fiction illusions.

Optical illusions have been studied for millenia. Even our prehistoric ancestors may have been puzzled by visual illusions, although they didn't leave traces of it. They surely must have noticed and experienced some visual phenomena such as: the after-image effect on their eyes when looking into the sun; a stick that seems broken when half of it is put in water; the Moon illusion (the rising Moon seems twice as large as the Moon in its zenith); and the natural optical phenomenon called a mirage.

The ancient Greeks used a technique known as *entasis* which incorporates a slight convexity in the columns of the Parthenon to compensate for the illusion of concavity created by parallel lines.

In English, there are two essential words to express the faculty and the act of seeing: "see" and "view." The etymological sense of the words "see" and "view" are "follow something with the eyes" (from the Indo-European *seq*) and "have learned" (from the Indo-European *weid*). So, for our ancestors, an image was something to shape with the eyes (follow with the eye) and information taken from the real world (having learned from this visual perception).

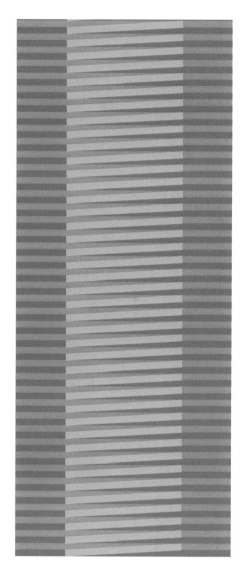

Just gray...
Color experiment with gray lines... What happens is called color assimilation: the gray color appears bluish in contact with blue, and orange-colored in contact with orange, giving the impression of a color gradation.

Unfortunately (or fortunately?), seeing isn't some kind of direct perception of reality. Atcually, our bairns are cnostanlty itnerperting, corrceting and gviing srtuctrues to the viusal ipnut form our eeys (see footnote below). If this were not the case, we wouldn't see any colors, and we would probably see the world upside down! We would also notice in our visual field a very large dot, called the blind spot, where the optic nerve enters the eye. Another interesting everyday paradox of our vision is that we don't see the edges of our visual field! In fact, we should see black zones outside of our visual field, but our brains cancel out these zones with a smooth, fade-out effect.

To resume, optical illusions teach us how we perceive things. But beyond the scientific aspect, they are great fun to look at! They can intrigue and entertain us. In this book, you will find a unique collection of visual puzzles to solve and optical illusions to explore, enjoy, and experiment with. In this book there are seven main types of illusion: ambiguous figures, impossible figures, hidden figures, color perception, moving patterns, paradoxes, and magic. This last topic includes true logic and visual paradoxes together with some neat mind bamboozlement. A large part of the illusions contained in this book were invented and designed by the authors, while some others are adaptations of lesser-known optical illusions or based on recent studies made by leading researchers in the field of cognitive neurosciences, such as E. Andelson, H. Ashida, J. Faubert, G. Kanisza, A. Kitaoka, A. Logvinenko, B. Pinna, and H. Van Tuijl.

Each illusion, when necessary, is explained with simple and clear words – this book is intended for everyone – but please be aware that most of the explanations are empirical and based on intuition rather than on real scientific proof. Some perceptive illusions are still under discussion and the scientists who studied these phenomena are only able to make suppositions. The best way to understand how and why an illusion works is to experience it with your friends and try constructing a variant. If the variant works, that means that you have understood the secret mechanism of the illusion. This book is a large compendium of new and interesting illusions and we hope that you will use our stunning illustrations as a resource and inspiration for designing and creating new optical illusions.

Most likely your brain has automatically corrected the sentence to, 'Actually, our brains are constantly interpreting, correcting and giving structure to the visual input from our eyes.' It's amazing, isn't it?

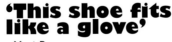

'This shoe fits like a glove'
— Yogi Berra

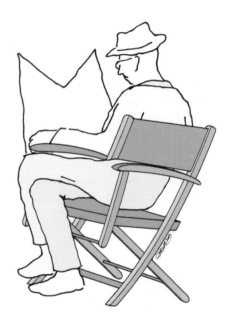

Tight position
Are you really looking at this man reading from behind? This is a kind of undecidable figure. The lower and upper part of the man seem to be in different directions.

FIGURE IT OUT (ambiguous and completion figures)

Does the mind represent the world accurately and unambiguously? Actually, ALL inputs to the brain are, to one degree or another, "ambiguous," allowing multiple interpretations. That's the reason why we have poets, artists, singers. The capacity to perceive and give different meanings to our environment is part of our human condition.

The most famous example of ambiguity in painting is the smile of the Mona Lisa by Leonardo da Vinci. In his book *The Story of Art*, Ernest Gombrich reports: 'Even in photographs of the painting we experience this strange effect, but in front of the original in the Paris Louvre it is almost uncanny. Sometimes she seems to mock at us, and then again we seem to catch something like sadness in her smile.' Ambiguous figures, also known as equivocal images or metamorphic images, are of special interest in the investigation of thinking. This is because they exemplify the fact that sometimes the same perceptual input can lead to very different representations, suggesting that the brain is actively involved in interpreting what we see, rather than passively recording it. The curious aspect of ambiguous figures is that once you have perceived both figures, it is impossible to focus on only one without the other popping into your vision from time to time. Our brain, in fact, resolves visual ambiguity by means of oscillation.

Ambiguous figures include figure-ground illusions, ambigrams, and what we will call completion figures. Figure-ground illusions are illusions that swap around the main figure and its background. Ambigrams are graphic words or sentences that can be read in more than one way. Completion figures are patterns which the mind rather unambiguously interprets in a particular way, despite the fact that the input is incomplete in relation to what is typically "perceived."

A certain style of completion figure, called droodles, was used in the late 1950s to entertain puzzle enthusiasts and magazine readers. These cartoons were rather abstract line drawings accompanied by an implicit question: 'what is it?' A punchline (usually a funny description), finally made the cartoons obvious. Completion figures and droodles are based on *pareidolia* (payr-eye-DOH-lee-uh), an innate human tendency to impose a pattern on random or ambiguous shapes. Astronomer Carl Sagan claimed that this tendency to see faces in tortillas, clouds, cinnamon buns, and the like is an evolutionary trait. He writes: 'As soon as the infant can see, it recognizes faces, and we now know that this skill is hardwired in our brains. Those infants who a million years ago were unable to recognize a face smiled back less, were less likely to win the hearts of their parents, and less likely to prosper. These days, nearly every infant is quick to identify a human face and to respond with a goony grin.' (Sagan, 1995).

Giving meaning to abstract forms can also be a way to exercise our visual thinking skills. Even da Vinci heartily recommended this method of invention as a practical technique for "opening the mind and putting it upon the scent of new thoughts." He once wrote: 'If you look upon an old wall covered with dirt or the

A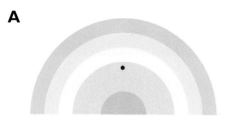

B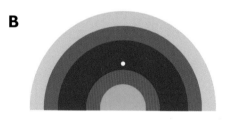

Brighten it up
The colors of the rainbow in A are faded. To restore their intensity, stare at the white dot in figure B for 20–30 seconds, then shift your gaze back to figure A. This effect is based on color adaptation.

odd appearance of some streaked stones, you may discover several things like landscapes, battles, clouds, uncommon attitudes, humorous faces, draperies...'

'A knife without a blade for which the handle is missing'

– G. C. Lichtenberg, in Göttingen Pocket Calendar.

THAT'S IMPOSSIBLE! (impossible figures)

When we observe a two-dimensional picture on paper, we often interpret it as a three-dimensional figure. This insistence on viewing objects as three-dimensional can lead to interesting perceptual problems.

An impossible object, also called an undecidable figure, is an object that cannot exist according to the known laws of physics but has a description or representation suggesting, at first sight, that it can be constructed. Generally, impossible objects depend on the ambiguous connectivity possible in line drawings. We like to call these improbable objects "Frankenstein figures" because they are made by matching together two or more different points of view of the same object, or by extending and blending together the perspective of one object with another one. Some impossible figures are not immediately obvious; you have to focus your attention on a particular zone of the representation of the object – the line of fusion of the contrasting perspectives – to understand that it cannot be realized. The paradox is that if you consider a sufficiently small zone of the drawing, the oddness disappears. That is to say, the "impossibility" is not here or there – it is something about the object as a whole. This paradox could perfectly illustrate the philosophical principle which says that, "The whole is something completely different from the sum of its parts."

The more the impossible object looks normal, the more it is fascinating! Impossible figures aren't created to baffle your eyes; their structure should appear coherent and logical. They are designed to confuse your mind. The "undecidability" of these figures invariably rests on them being interpreted as two-dimensional projections of what would be an impossible higher-dimensional object. Artist Maurice Escher is notable for many drawings that feature undecidable figures, sometimes the entire drawing being an impossible figure. Oscar Reutersvärd, another important artist, has conducted a lifelong exploration into the world of impossible figures, producing a prodigious body of work during his long career.

Notable modern undecidable figures include:

– impossible cube
– Penrose stairs
– Penrose triangle
– blivet (or Devil's Pitchfork)

We should not forget to add Mickey Mouse's ears to the list. Yes, his ears do not follow the basic rules of perspective.

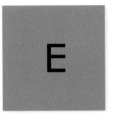 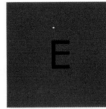

Quick color eyesight test

Close one eye and stare at the two colored squares each containing the letter E. If one of the E's seems darker you may need a pair of glasses! Do the test with the other eye too. This test is based on the chromatic aberration of the lens in our eye, making red colors focus slightly behind the retina and green colors slightly in front. In normal conditions, chromatic aberration passes unnoticed, but a slight nearsightedness or farsightedness increases the irregularity, making a color go over the edges of a letter E.

Children and adults alike are so accustomed to the current aspect of this cartoon character that they don't notice at all that his ears are actually impossible figures! But impossible figures have a long history. In 1025, an unknown European artist unintentionally drew the first example of impossible figure art (three impossible pillars), in a painting *Madonna a Gyermekkel* ("Madonna and Child – Adoration of the Magi"). Another example of an impossible artistic object (a gallows!) was painted by Pieter Brueghel in *Magpie on the Gallows* (1568). However, the first artist who "deliberately" misuses perspective to create an absurd and impossible landscape is the famous English artist William Hogarth (1697-1764) whose artwork *Perspective Absurdities* formed the frontispiece to J. J. Kirby's book *Dr. Brook Taylor's Method of Perspective Made Easy in Both Theory and Practice* (1754). This book was intended to teach people how to draw in perspective, so the caption asserted: 'Whoever makes a design without the knowledge of perspective will be liable to such absurdities as are shown in this frontispiece.'

'Three things cannot be long hidden: the sun, the moon, and the truth'

– Gautama Siddharta, the founder of Buddhism.

FIND THE OBJECT (hidden objects)

In France, prints called *images d'Epinal* were given to children by grocers as a premium gift. These cards depicted traditional scenes of everyday life, historical facts, legends or visual riddles, and were popular in the latter half of the 1800s and in the early 1900s. The object of these puzzling cards was often to find a hidden image (or several hidden images) within a picture. At that time, children were delighted when they found the latent image hidden in the manifest image. This innocent mental process is related to the concept of the lost object used in psychoanalysis. Finding the object "is just a process of retrieving something that is already there," asserted Freud.

Since then, hidden-figure puzzles have been appreciated worldwide by puzzle enthusiasts. The principle is still the same. A hidden-figure puzzle is mostly a single image accompanied by a caption below it. The text, one or two lines long, introduces the image and indicates the object to be found in the drawing: an animal, a human being, a geometric shape, and so on. The image should then be turned in every direction to find the hiding-place of the subject.

Basically, hidden image puzzles are also optical illusions because they bring into play the foreground and background relationships of our visual perception. The term pregnance (from the German word "Prägnanz") is applied in psychology to explain the tendency to distinguish certain objects from their background. Some shapes, like discs, have the property of being more easily detected than other ones, even when they are incomplete or

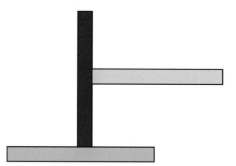

Yellow rod = green rod?
The rods form the Chinese character 'high.' Are the yellow and green rods of the same length? They are – measure them!

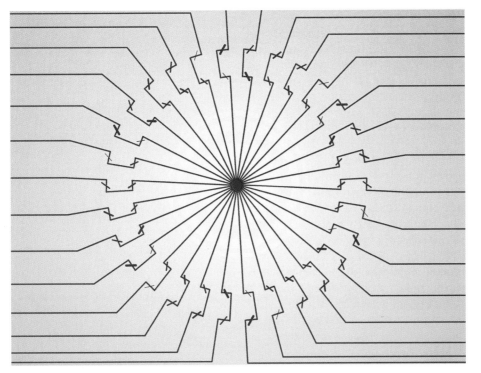

Follow my eyes

Stare at the center of the geometric picture shown here. Keeping your gaze fixed on the central blue spot, move your head backwards and forwards several times. What happens? The blue concentric circles appear to rotate in opposite directions!

Photocopy the optical illusion and paste it on a rectangular piece of cardboard. Then, keeping the image 30 cm away from your eyes, give a swinging movement. What do you see now? The concentric circles seem to expand or shrink, like the aperture of a camera, depending on the swinging direction you give to the image.

surrounded by a large quantity of other forms. But this isn't as natural or evident as you may think, and this will be demonstrated by the tests you'll encounter on the following pages. Normally, your brain 'reads' your visual field like a book, trying to discriminate the meaningful letters (objects) from the meaningless page (background). This process of distinction is not always easy, as there are elements that can cause 'noise' which is the result of an over-abundance of images, misperception, or deliberate camouflage and encryption. Hidden figures are widely used in neuropsychological tests to measure figure-ground discrimination. These tests are called Embedded Figures Tests (EFT). Why not do the tests on the following pages? You can do them alone or with your friends. The time allocated to resolve each picture is five minutes. Those who score highly are described as being field-independent, and have ability to "distinguish the message from the noise," while those who find it difficult to find the hidden shapes are called field-dependent and have a greater tendency to perceive complete patterns rather than their separate components.

The secret to solving hidden figures lies in losing yourself in the whole scene, and not in a particular area that seems at first glance to have more probability of hiding the figure than another area. Don't act like the drunken man searching for his keys within the beam of light below a streetlamp, who answered a helpful passerby enquiring if he was sure that he had lost them within the beam of light; 'No, of course not; it's dark over there.'

'I often think that the night is more alive and more richly colored than the day'

– Vincent Van Gogh

COLOR COORDINATION?
(color and brightness effects)

We have a secret we want to share with you. Color doesn't exist at all in nature! Color only starts to exist when our perception systems produce the impression of 'color.' Light is perceived on the retina as a stimulus and is processed into a perception of color in our brain. In substance, colors are already illusions in themselves. Color serves a special function in the processes of vision. Our ability to analyze and process colors is a result of having three types of cone receptors in the retina, which have different light wavelength sensitivities. Sure, the eye is not a perfect optical instrument due to possible chromatic aberration of the lens, yellowing with age, and variations of sensitivity. But, coupled with the brain, human vision is satisfactorily reliable and constant. In certain situations, some of the effects that the brain uses to enhance vision can be observed. These include after-image, assimilation, changing color sensibilities, chromatic aberration, retinal rivalry, retreating and advancing colors, lightness constancy, simultaneous contrast, and the influence of color on apparent size and weight. Color adaptation or assimilation is

Continuous lines?
Are the oblique lines in the square continuous from side to side? No, but you have to take a closer look at the pattern in order to realize it.

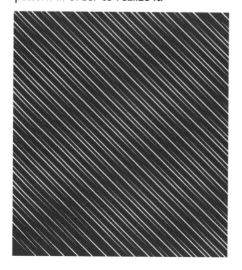

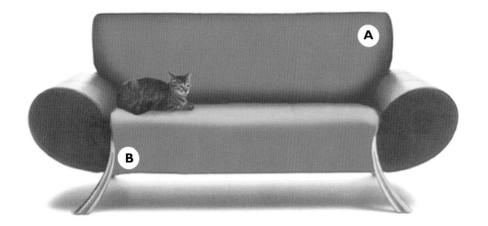

Grey sofa

Is the gray zone in a) darker than the gray zone in b)? The gray zones in a) and b) have exactly the same hue. We tend to perceive the gray zone in a) to be darker. This experiment shows that the perceived brightness doesn't rely only on the amount of light that reaches the eye from the observed object.

the tendency of the eye to adapt in seconds to most prevailing light sources. Because of this effect, the eye can, in turn, accurately identify the colors of objects under changing lighting conditions. Adaptation will be seen by a person traveling in a vehicle with tinted windows; if, for instance, the tint is blue, the landscape will at first seem suffused with a blue cast, but as the eye quickly desensitizes itself to blue, the view will soon reassume its normal coloration.

Lightness constancy: objects that are viewed under different lighting conditions usually "look" the same to us. For example, a white T-shirt will look the same whether it is brightly lit on a sunny day or dimly lit on an overcast day. This is despite the fact that the wavelength of light that reaches the retinas in each case is different. This is explained by the fact that the brightness of an object's surroundings usually change in proportion to the change in brightness of the object itself.

After-image is a negative or complementary 'ghost' of a color seen after prolonged stimulation of the eye. An after-image occurs by staring first at a black spot on a white surface for around 20 seconds; then, shifting one's gaze to a black surface, a floating white spot will be seen briefly. The after-image of a red spot would be blue-green, that of a blue one would be yellow-orange, and that of a violet spot would be greenish-yellow. After-image effects involve the optic nerves. An optical nerve is composed of millions of neuronal fibers which connect the retina to the brain by decoding the stimuli of the retina into three different signals: light difference (black/white) or luminance, red/green color difference, and blue/yellow color difference. When you stare at a red square for 20 seconds or more, the cells of the optic nerve, those which transmit the presence of red AND the absence of green will be under tension and will be saturated; consequently, when the stimulus suddenly disappears, the brain will interpret this stimulus cut effectively as the absence of red AND the presence of green. A green square will therefore appear in your visual field. It's like a short flip-flop effect. Interestingly, most standards for television transmission use a very similar decoding system with one luminance and two chrominance channels. A curious effect called retinal rivalry may be obtained by stimulating both retinas, each with a different color. For instance, when a blue glass is placed before one eye and a yellow or red one before the other, the two independent monocular fields fight for supremacy; vision appears alternately in one color and then the other, and the brain has great trouble resolving the images. (This is not a problem associated with 3-D motion pictures!) Simultaneous color contrast is an effect in which the contrast between adjacent colors is enhanced by the eye. The effect is particularly strong with a pair of complementary colors, such as red and green or orange and blue. If these colors are put together in tight patterns, the resulting contrast is so strong that flickering will occur and the eye may experience considerable discomfort. Simultaneous lightness contrast is an effect in which a color of given brightness will look darker on a light background and brighter on a dark background. Simultaneous contrasts depend on lateral inhibition of our visual system. Some photoreceptors of the retina are activated when they detect light, while others are activated in the absence of light. These two types usually encircle each other and are spread throughout the retina, creating receptive fields. Often, light can fall on to both light and dark photoreceptors, causing the two regions to compete with one another. One part of the receptive field wants to become active while the other part does not. This competitive interaction is called lateral inhibition. Because of this antagonistic nature of receptive fields, perceptual illusions, such as the Herman or Lingelbach grid illusion, can occur when we look at certain patterns containing contrasting colors. Since warm (reddish) colors tend to advance and cold (bluish) colors tend to recede in our visual field, objects painted in red and orange will seem to be slightly larger than those painted in the cool blues and greens. Red cars or buses may seem larger than they actually are, but a room painted in red will seem more confined than a blue one. The reason for these effects is chromatic aberration, a problem associated with lenses (including the one used to focus light in the human eye) in which light is refracted by different amounts according to its wavelength. As a result, yellow is the only color perfectly focused by the normal eye, with red focused slightly behind the retina and blue slightly in front. The second reason may be that associative elements come into play. For example, blue may seem to recede because of the association it has in our memory with distance (the sky, sea, distant mountains). The value (relative lightness or darkness) of a color also affects our perception of the weight of an object. In the following pages you will experience some effects related to color, including color and lightness illusions, neon color spreading effect, scintillating grid effect, Kanisza illusion, Boynton filling-in phenomenon and more.

'Things are not what they seem; nor are they otherwise'

– excerpt from *Lankavatara Sutra.*

IN THE MIND'S EYE
(length, size and shape misperception)

Our brain often translates the physical image we perceive into an image which is more useful to our senses. As you experience it in everyday life, there is a distinction between the actual size of an object, its apparent size, and its imaginary size. The actual size of an object cannot be observed, because in order for our eyes to focus upon that object, it must be at a certain distance. But you can calculate or measure it. The apparent size of an object depends on several factors described below. A camel may not pass through the eye of a needle, but its image – apparent size – can. Actually, it would be possible to see through a 2mm wide eye of a needle, a 2m (6.6 ft) wide camel placed at a distance of 1km (3281 ft) from you. What about the imaginary size? Psychologically, we tend to see objects larger (or smaller) than they appear in reality. For example, it's very difficult to determine at a rough guess the real size of circular objects.

The fact that we have two eyes (binocular vision) is more than sufficient to provide information on distances, and for that reason we don't need three. One of these binocular distance cues is called convergence. Convergence refers to the turning-in of our eyes as objects come closer to our eyes (and is what causes you to squint!). The other thing that happens as objects come closer is that our visual accommodation changes.

Another cue to distance perception, especially for more complex scenes in which there are multiple objects, is binocular disparity. That means that each eye records a different angle of the visual field. Yet another cue to distance is motion parallax. As you move from one location to another, objects at various distances will move in a direction dependent on where you are fixating. Finally, it turns out that color and brightness can also have an effect on how far away something appears.

The perceived or apparent size of objects depends primarily on the visual angle subtended by the object on the retina in our eyes. All other things being equal, the object that subtends the larger visual angle will appear larger. The visual angle is dependent on the real size of the object and on the distance the object is from our eyes.

Another factor affecting perceived size is size constancy. This phenomenon results in objects of known size tending to appear constant in size regardless of their actual distance. So, for example, if you are looking at your friend and that friend starts walking away from you, the friend does not, at the same time, start to appear smaller even though the visual angle subtended by that friend is getting less and less. Well, size constancy also depends on distance, and if it is large enough, known objects will appear smaller. If you have ever looked down at the ground from a very tall building, you will have noticed that people on the sidewalks and cars in the streets look very small. Perspective also plays a part in perception of size.

In conclusion, despite our ability to judge distance and size differences in many cases, our ability is distorted by a wide range of subjective factors. What is really interesting is that size illusions affect only the visual

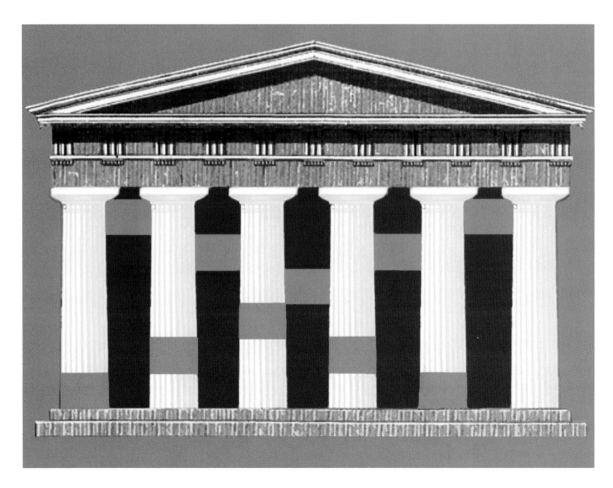

Temple of colors
Examine the pale purple rectangles on the Greek temple. Are they of the same shade, or do some rectangles appear darker than other ones? The pale purple rectangles are all the same hue. Objects tend to be darker when placed on a clear, luminous background and vice versa.

perception, but not the senses which control our organs of motion. Thus, scientists presume that there are two kinds of visual connections, one directly concerning visual perception and the other involving motory control.

Let's talk about illusions. If the mother of all illusions in size perception is the Müller-Lyer illusion – published in the prestigious journal *Archiv für Anatomie und Physiologie* in 1889 – the father is the Ponzo illusion. We can say that all modern illusions on size distortion are based on these two contributions. The Müller-Lyer and Ponzo illusions are clearly related to the effect of perspective. In the Müller-Lyer illusion, the fins and the arrows at both ends of the lines provide a sensation of receding and advancing corners; in the Ponzo illusion, the angle of the converging lines in the background creates apparent depth through linear perspective.

In this book we will explore some of the things that affect our ability to estimate comparative lengths, sizes, and shapes, and examine some geometrical properties that induce those deformations. We will also take into consideration the so-called alignment illusions and perceptive distortions, whereby repeating regular background patterns can so strongly dominate other regular geometric shapes placed onto them that they appear distorted (not aligned or parallel, bulging or swelling).

'Eppur si muove!' (But it does move!)

MOVING PARTS (illusory moving patterns)

How is it possible to create the illusion of motion with geometric and static images? There is a branch of modern art named Op Art (short for "Optic art") which is concerned with such optic effects. Op Art paintings often play with optic interference and moiré to create illusory colors and motion. The precursor of the Op Art was Victor Vasarely, a Hungarian artist. But Bridget Riley is perhaps the best known of the Op artists. Taking Vasarely's lead, she painted a number of works consisting only of black and white lines. Riley's paintings depict an unreal geometric world which frequently gives the impression of movement or color.

Apparent motion illusions are based on alternating optical contrasts (clear/dark, vertical/horizontal, left/right) to create a perturbation, a visual overload perturbing the retinal circuits, which can, among other things, make our eyesight flicker.

Until now, we can count roughly four different families of relative movement or kinetic effects: phantom movements like moving flows, scintillating, and popping-up patterns; floating images (such as the Ouchi illusion), rotating shapes (the B. Pinna and G. Brelstaff illusion), and self-moving and spontaneous rotating shapes (peripheral drift illusion). Let's go deeper into two of these.

Pinna rotating illusion

The Pinna-Brelstaff rotating illusion consists of two (or more) concentric rings of slanted lines or geometric shapes. When an observer moves towards the display the two rings of geometric patterns appear to counter-rotate. The illusion is optimal when there is a 66 degree orientation difference between elements composing the inner and outer rings. Three factors may cause this illusion: the luminance profile and the angular direction of the shapes, and the bad integration of motion signals in our brain.

The peripheral drift illusion

This illusion was first described by the scientists A. Fraser and K. Wilcox, and by J. Faubert. The most famous peripheral drift illusion designed by A. Kitaoka is called Rotating Snakes. It consists of concentric repeating patterns of white, yellow, black and blue which evoke a striking illusion of motion. What makes this illusion so interesting is the fact that you are experiencing movement in the periphery, although you realize that the moving objects are not moving at all! While peripheral vision demonstrates movement over the entire field of the display, focusing on one particular part of the illusion shows that it is stationary. There are no definite answers to explain this phenomenon, but the main characteristics of the illusion are:

1 Illusory motion appears from a black region to the adjacent dark-gray region or from a white region to the adjacent light-gray region. Colors indicating the directions of illusory motion: black to dark gray or white to light gray.

2 It occurs well in peripheral vision. The object we fixate on appears to be stationary.

3 It occurs well with stimuli of edges. Stimuli of smooth luminance profiles give weak illusions.

4 It occurs well with fragmented or curved edges. Stimuli made up of long edges give weak illusions.

5 It may be generated by involuntary, halting eye movements.

Some apparent movement illusions contained in this book work better on a computer screen (because of the luminance), so you can try scanning them and watching them on your PC. You can also use these illusions as a resource or inspiration to design new illusory moving patterns. If you find a new pattern or a new way to enhance illusory motion, it would be great to hear from you!

'Mr. Speaker, I withdraw my statement that half the cabinet are asses. Half the cabinet are not asses'

— Benjamin Disraeli

RIGHT OR WRONG? (the paradox of images)

Optical illusions can be useful to interest people in exploring and following logic and mathematical topics. On the following pages, we will present some "impossible" or paradoxical perception puzzles and self-working visual trick puzzles based on misconceptions and misperception. This means you'll be able to experience the persuasive powers of the images and learn how a picture can sidetrack your senses of reasoning! We will also take the opportunity to deal with self-referential images and graphic words.

What exactly are vanish puzzles? Vanish puzzles (we've renamed them "stereophanic puzzles") have existed for five centuries, but they still continue to amaze everyone! They can be of two types: figurative vanish puzzles and geometric vanish puzzles. Figurative

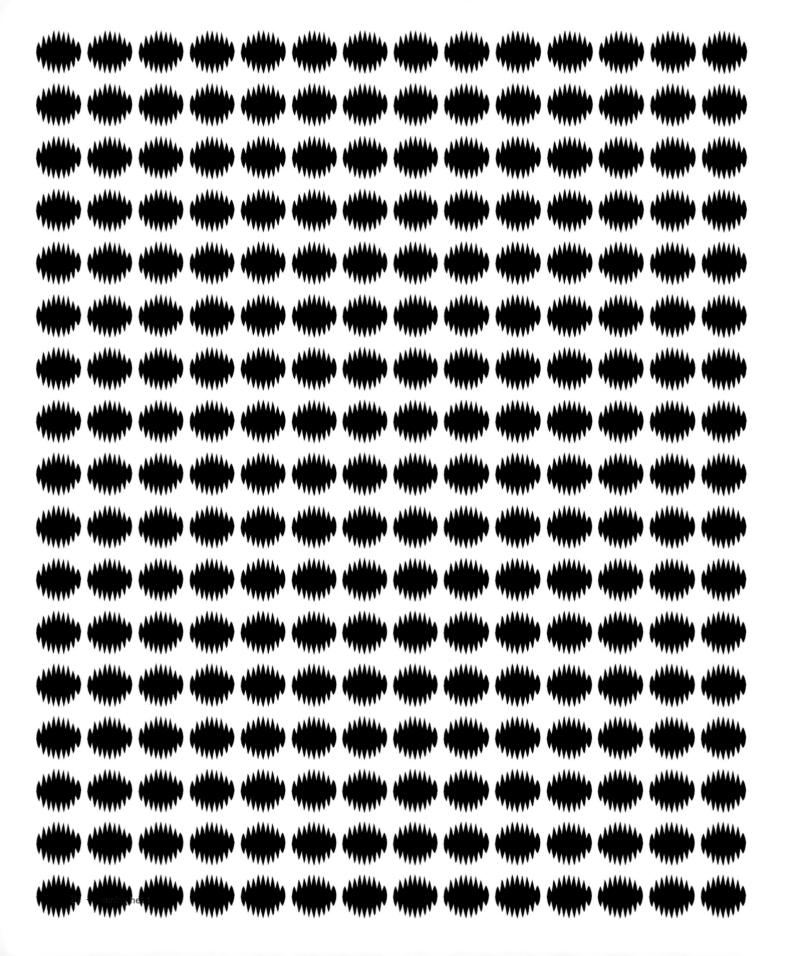

vanish puzzles involve the rearranging of parts of a puzzle representing a scene with a series of elements (people, animals, etc.) so that once the rearrangement is complete, an element of the scene disappears (or reappears). Geometric vanish puzzles involve either the apparent disappearance of a part of their surface or an apparent reducing of their area when the pieces of the puzzles are rearranged.

The first example of vanishing area puzzles was discovered in the book *Libro d'Architettura Primo* by Sebastiano Serlio, an Italian architect of the Renaissance, even though Serlio didn't notice that any area had actually vanished! The first description and explanation of this paradox was found in a math puzzle book with a long title: *Rational Recreations in which the Principles of Numbers and Natural Philosophy are Clearly and Copiously Elucidated, by a Series of Easy, Entertaining, Interesting Experiments among which are all those Commonly Performed with the Cards* (1774) by William Hooper.

Because of their visual impact, vanish puzzles are really striking, but their mechanism is quite simple: the part (figure, surface) which disappears is simply redistributed differently on the remaining parts of the puzzle, confirming Lavoisier's law which says, 'In nature, nothing is created, nothing is lost, all is transformed.' Then, the magic is only based on the visual persuasion that the puzzle is really different after manipulation. Well, vanish puzzles are just one aspect of perception puzzles. In this book, you will find some new games and magic tricks directly involving visual perception or visual memory.

A self-reference occurs when an object refers to itself. Reference is possible when there are two logical levels of interpretation which can sometimes interfere with each other (contradiction). So, self-referential statements can lead to paradoxes. Many self-referential paradoxes are hidden in our everyday life. They are like optical illusions; they seem normal, but when you examine them closely, the incongruities become obvious!

On the following pages, we have prepared a small selection of intriguing, visual self-reference puzzles for you that are guaranteed to raise a smile if you give them enough thought. Do we have any doubt about that? Well, yes and no…

So dive in and enjoy some fantastic optical illusions! And if you get stuck, there are answers and explanations at the end of each gallery.

Blackout (left)

You may see hues of colors on the background of this pattern. Interestingly, if you scan this pattern in high-resolution color, your scanner will also reproduce colors! This effect occurs because the alternating small black and white spokes give intermittent stimulation to color receptors in our retina. Sometimes these stimuli interfere with each other, producing a subjective color illusion.

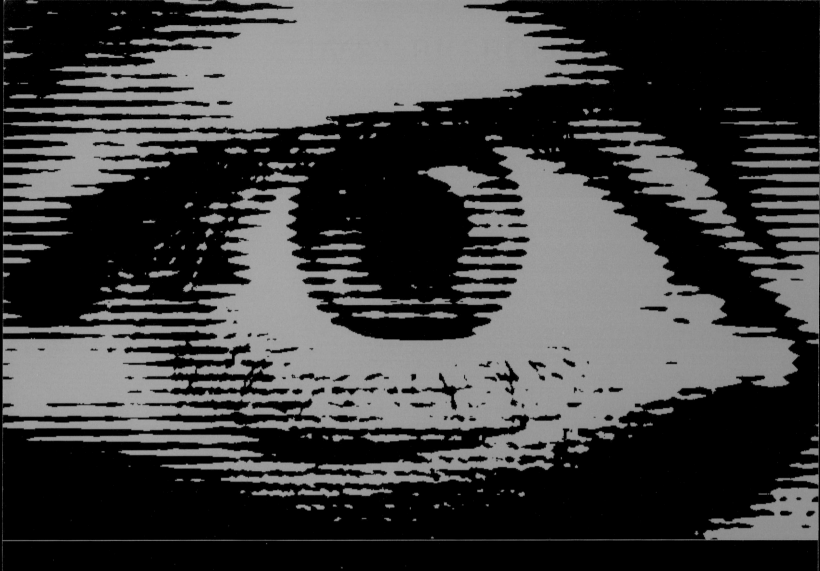

Gallery 1

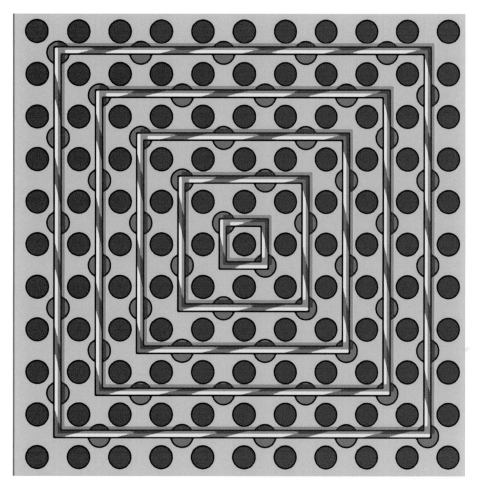

Tilting squares

Are the squares really tilting to the left? No; they are all perfectly upright squares. The illusion is induced by the alternating orders of red and blue dots on the background.

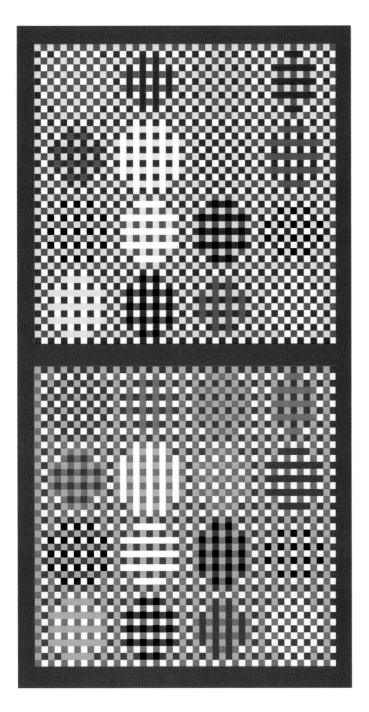

Pixelling

With only three colors, plus black and white, we can create a huge variety of apparent colors due to color contrast and color assimilation effects. The first table is composed of primary colors (red, blue and yellow); the second one, of secondary colors (green, violet, orange). View the tables from a certain distance to see the effects. Primary colors can create apparent secondary colors such as orange and green; whereas secondary colors can create primary colors such as blue or yellow.

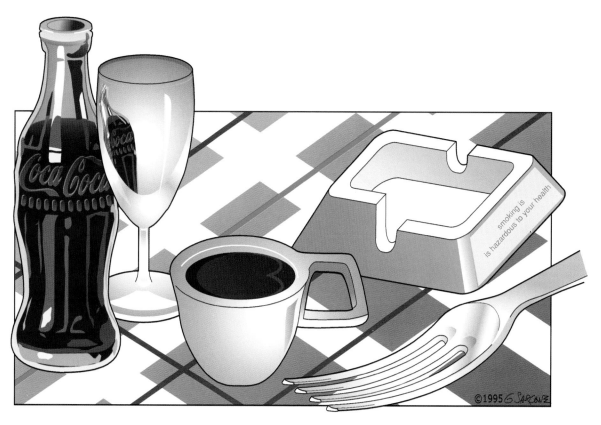

Restaurant oddities
Find six critical errors in the picture! (Answer on page 44.)

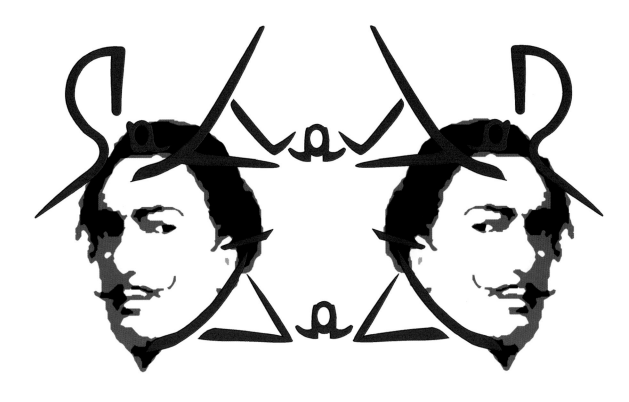

Dali forever
Place the image in front of a mirror. What do you observe? (Answer on page 44.)

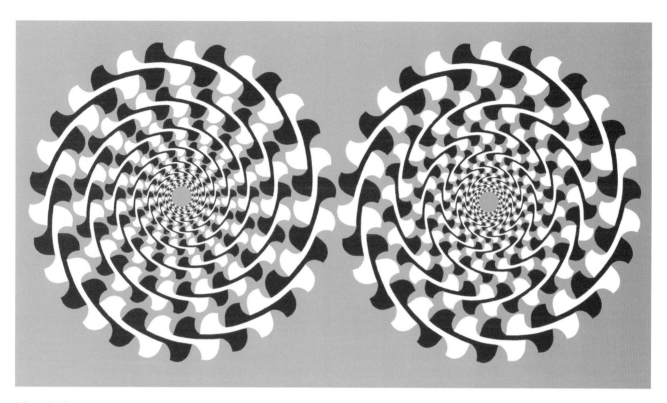

Unspiral

Which one of these figures is a spiral?

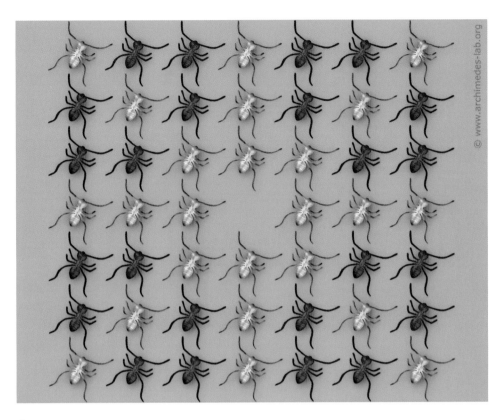

Ant square

At a glance, would you say there are more red ants or white ants?

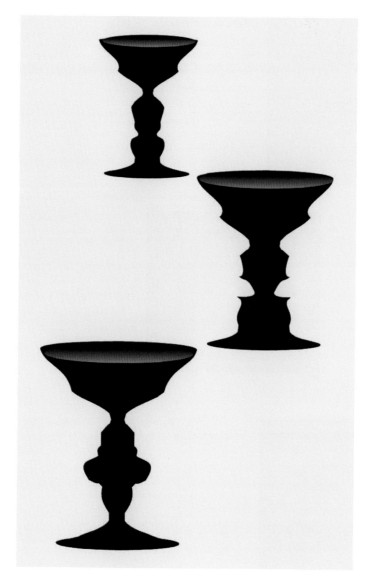

Talking cups

These cups are telling the story of an unexpected encounter. Can you summarize it?

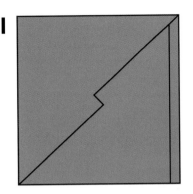

Paradoxical hole
Explain why, when three pieces of the square shown in fig. 1 are arranged as illustrated in fig. 3, we obtain the same square but with a mysterious hole!

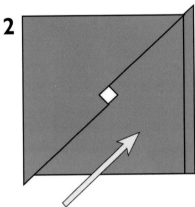

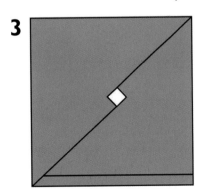

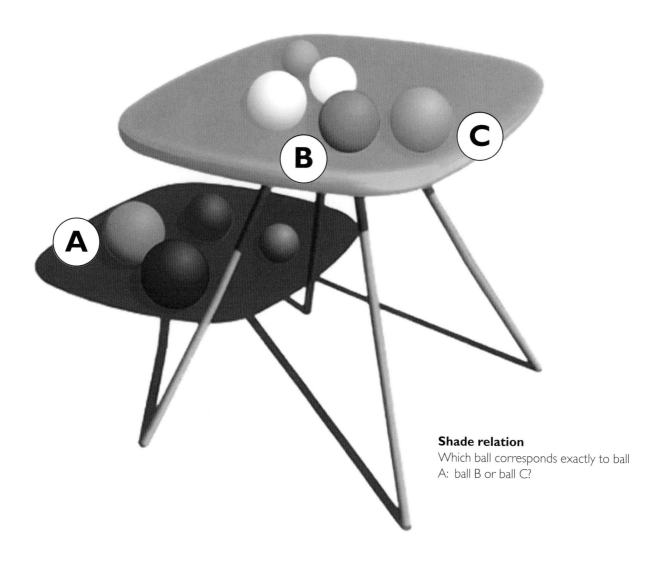

Shade relation
Which ball corresponds exactly to ball
A: ball B or ball C?

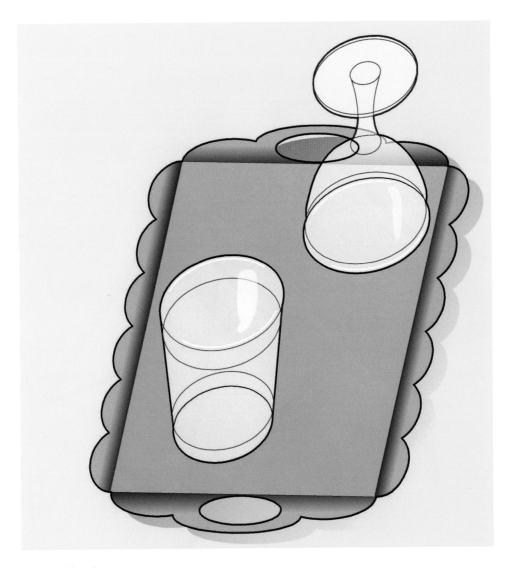

Magic Glass?
Find a way to remove one of the glasses from the tray completely.

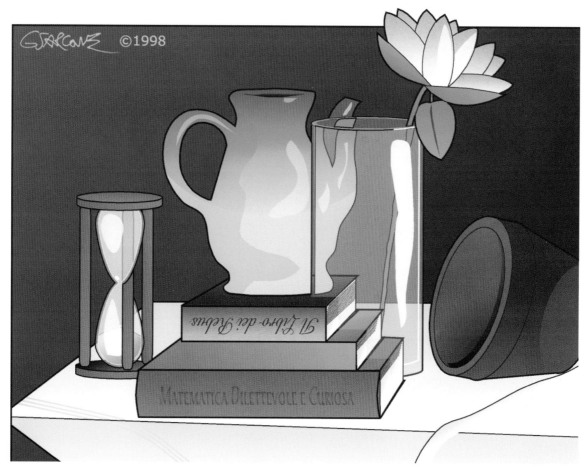

More oddities
Spot four oddities in the picture!

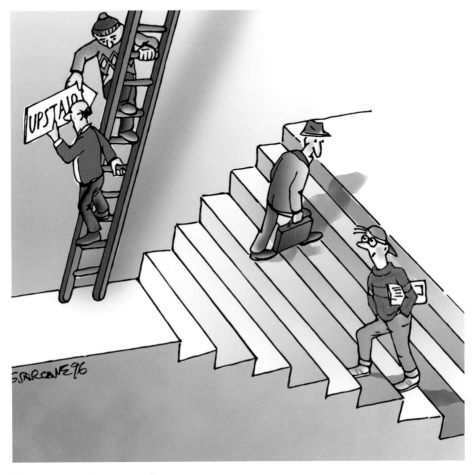

Every way takes you up!
You can go up in two opposite directions on these magic stairs...

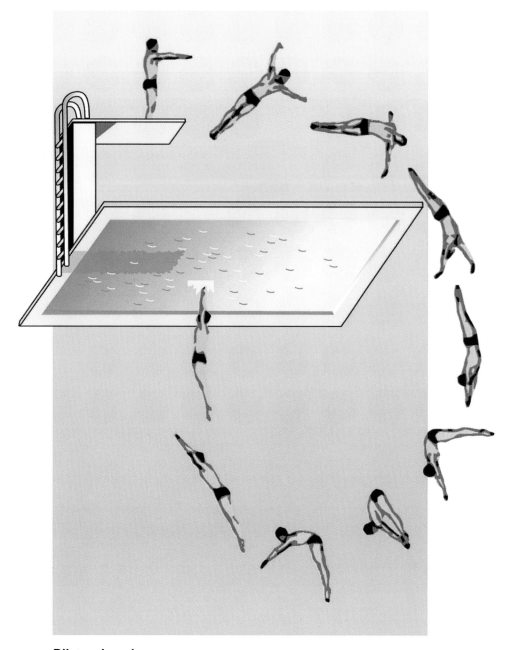

Bilateral pool
The diver makes a jump into the fourth dimension and enters the water from the underside (turn the page upside-down).

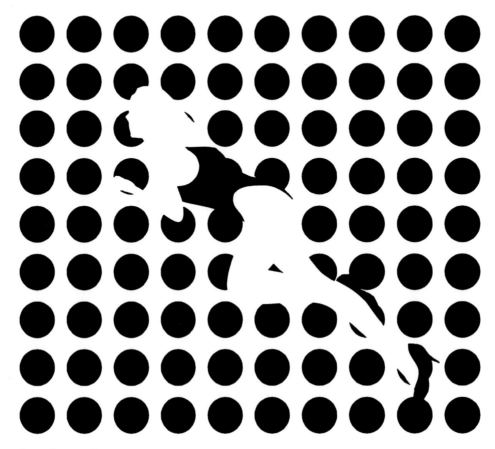

Imaginary pin-up
I bet some of you wish this pin-up girl was really there! Sorry, it's just your imagination...

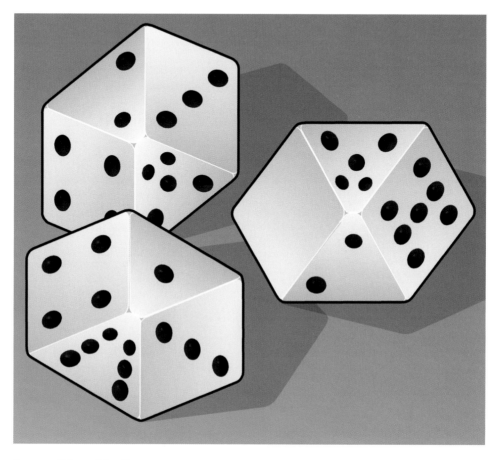

Impossible cubic dice

These are unreal four-dimensional, eight-sided die (the eight sides are numbered by dots from 0 to 7, strategically placed so that the sum of the dots on opposite sides equals 7).

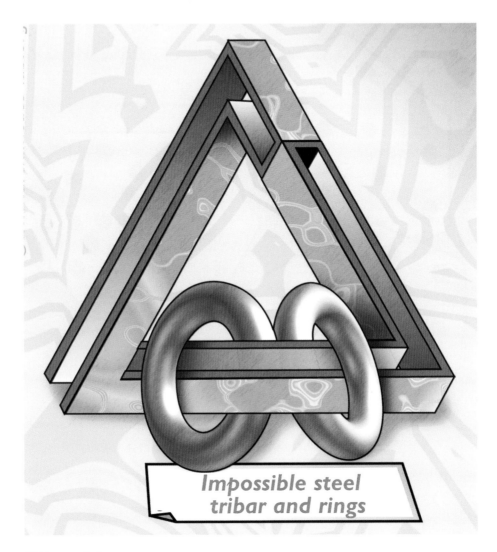

Impossible steel
tribar and rings

Tribar and rings
A 'classic' impossible tribar with two strange rings slipped onto one
of its bars. As you can see, the rings are perspectively incoherent.

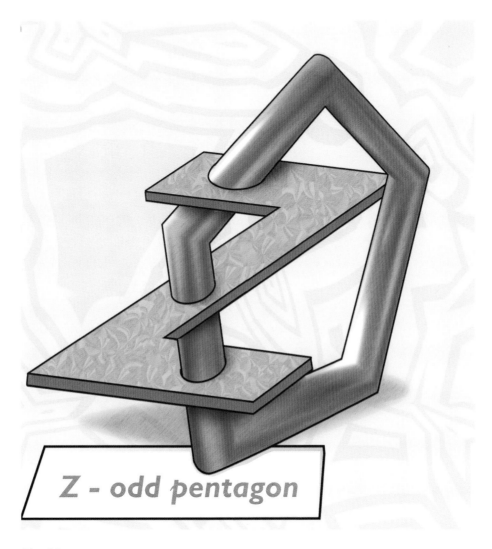

Z-odd pentagon

The Z-shaped board intersects the pentagon at three impossible points.

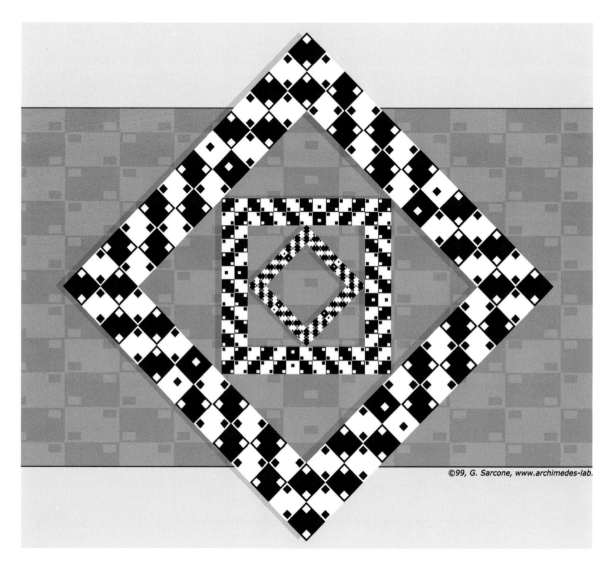

Distorted?

Is anything in the picture straight?

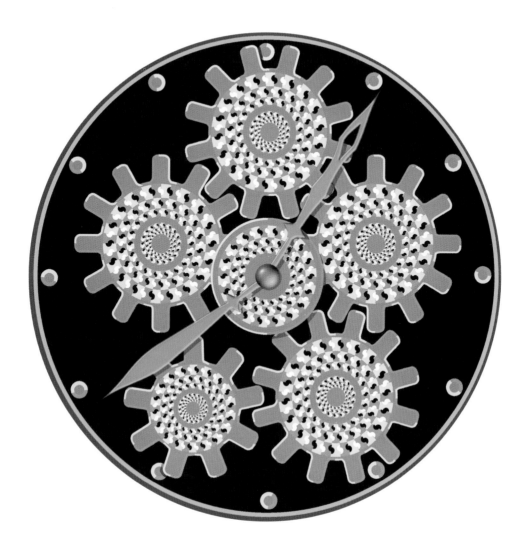

Apparent rotations

Move your eyes around the clock and the gears will appear to rotate. Circular objects, including radial repeating patterns with "sawtooth" luminance profiles, produce a sensation of motion called peripheral drift illusion. A. Kitaoka, a Japanese perception scientist, specializes in designing such illusory patterns (you can see his work at: http://www.psy.ritsumei.ac.jp/~akitaoka/). However, this kind of illusion works even better when it is sufficiently enlarged or seen on a computer screen.

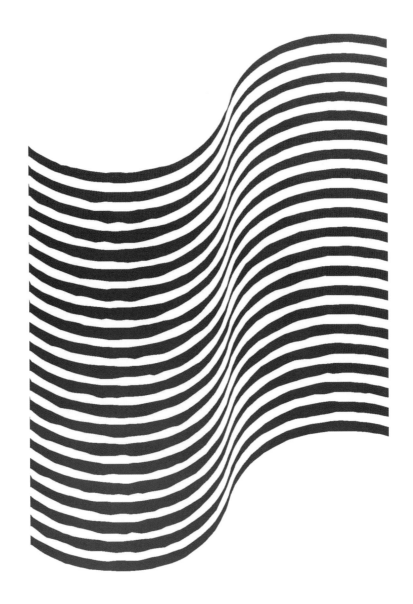

A tribute to da Vinci
Leonardo's face is hidden in the stripes – can you see it?

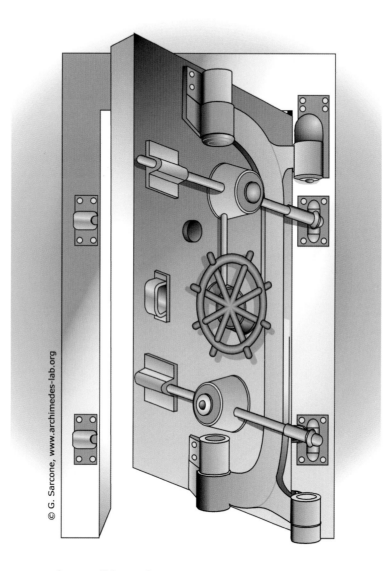

Impossible vault
Push or pull? Your money wouldn't be safe in this vault!

Gallery 1 Notes

Page 25
1 The Coca-Cola (Coca-Coca) logo on the bottle.
2 The top of the glass stands in front of the bottle while the stem is behind.
3 The writing on the ashtray contains "is" twice: Smoking is is hazardous to your health.
4 The ashtray has an impossible geometric shape.
5 The handle of the coffee cup.
6 The teeth of the fork (are there three or four teeth? Maybe both!).

Page 26
This image looks the same when seen in the mirror! This kind of word is called a reflection ambigram. A surprising number of words offer this type of symmetry when written, such as: TOOT, MOM, etc.

Page 27
Neither of them, because they're both perfect concentric circles!

Page 28
You've probably answered that there are more white ants as they are more scattered throughout the picture... the ants are, however, equal in number! Another illusion is that the square made up of ants seems to tilt slightly to the left.

Page 29
In the profile of the first cup (in the background) you can see the faces of two frowning people who meet each other unexpectedly. In the second cup, we can see that they are sticking out their tongues at each other; and finally, in the third cup, they laugh and go off to have a drink together. Maybe they were old friends!

Page 30
If you could stack square A on the top of 'square' B, you'd see a tiny difference (in red). This difference represents the area of the hole in 'square' B. So nothing disappeared, the missing piece is just redistributed in the whole area of 'square' B ('square' B isn't actually a square, but a rectangle).

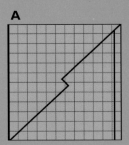
A

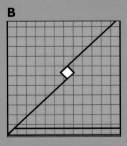
B

Page 31
Ball B, even if it seems darker than ball A. This is a simultaneous lightness contrast effect.

Page 32
Just turn the image upside-down and the wine glass will be seen standing outside the tray. Amazing, isn't it? This image was invented by Gianni Sarcone for a science festival on optical illusions.

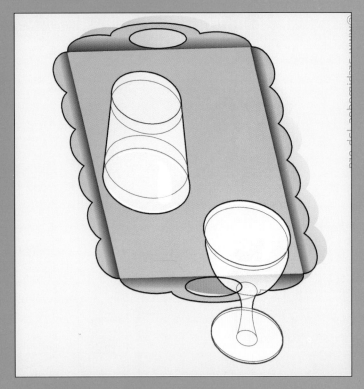

Page 33
1 The upper part of the hourglass is outside the rung, the lower part is behind it.
2 The top of the transparent vase stands in front of the pitcher while the bottom is behind the books.
3 The bottom of the vase on the right doesn't correspond perspectively to its opening.
4 The books appear to be two or three at the same time.

Page 40
The checkered frames are perfectly straight. The small white and black squares create layouts of 'subliminal' oblique lines which interfere with the orthogonal outlines of the frames creating the bulging illusion. If you observe the picture with half-closed eyes, you can perceive these

'subliminal' oblique lines similar to the blurred figure below. This is a neat version of the Zölner illusion.

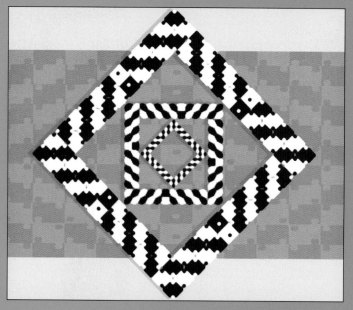

Page 42
To see the three-dimensional face of da Vinci, view the image from a distance of six feet (two meters). Each stripe contains a small portion of information about Leonardo's face. Our brain gathers and interprets all this partial information and then assembles it as one unique image.

Page 43
This is an impossible figure illusion: the lower side of the reinforced door is opening away from you, while the upper side is opening towards you.

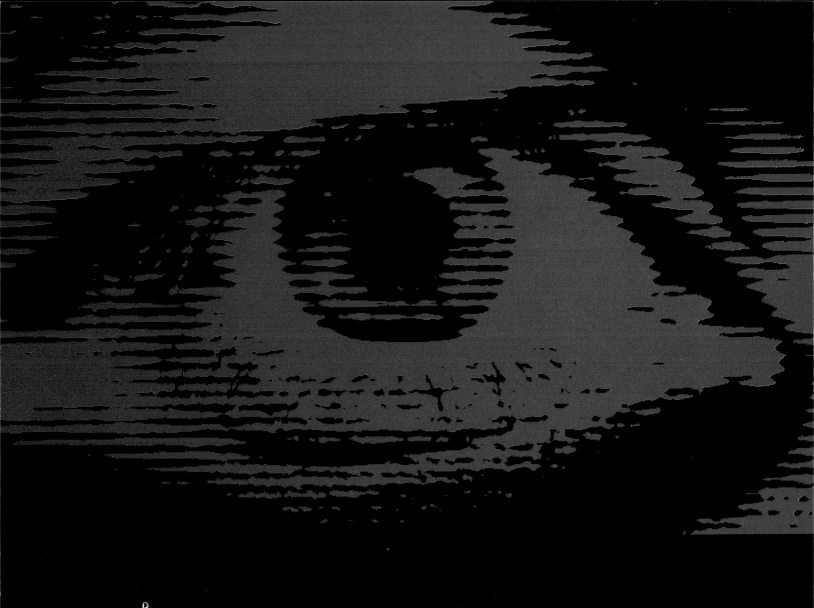

Gallery II

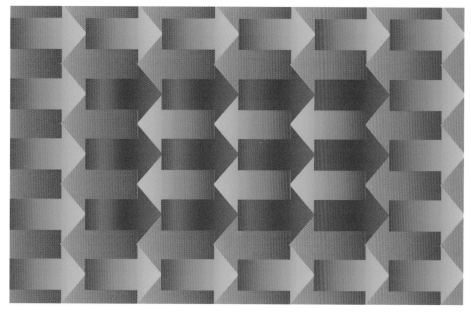

Ambiguous arrows
Figure-ground ambiguity.

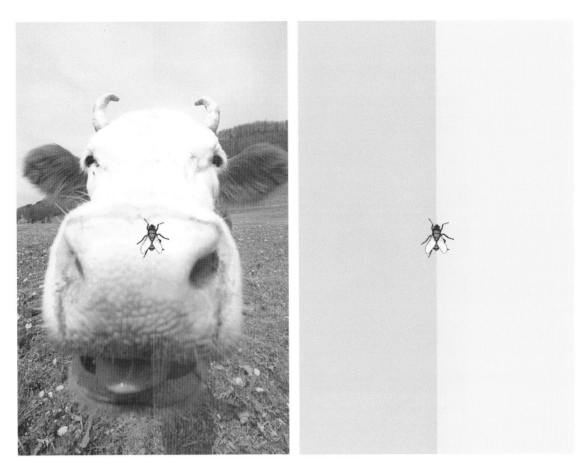

Off-color cow
The color in this photograph of a cow is not balanced at all
(the left side is bluish and the right side has too much yellow).
To restore the balance, stare at the fly in the second diagram for
thirty seconds, then look at the cow again.

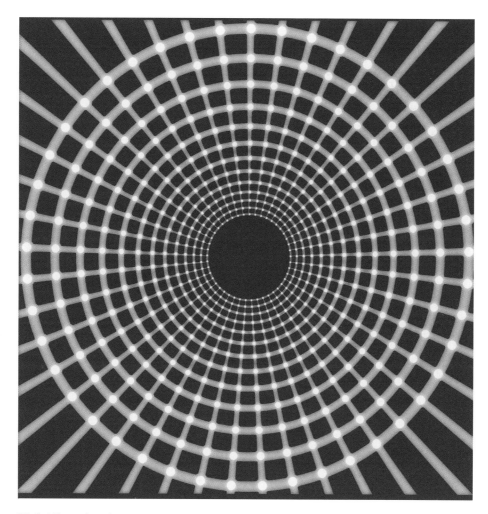

Twinkling circular pattern

In the above illustration, dark brown dots appear to form and vanish at the intersections of the gray circles and spokes when you scan your eyes across the image.

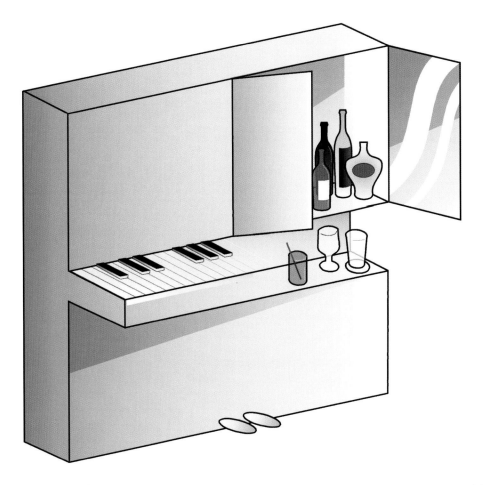

Real piano bar
An impossible scene for night revelers.

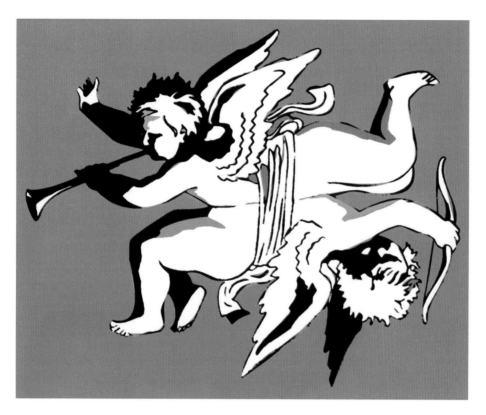

How many angels?

How many angels are in the picture?

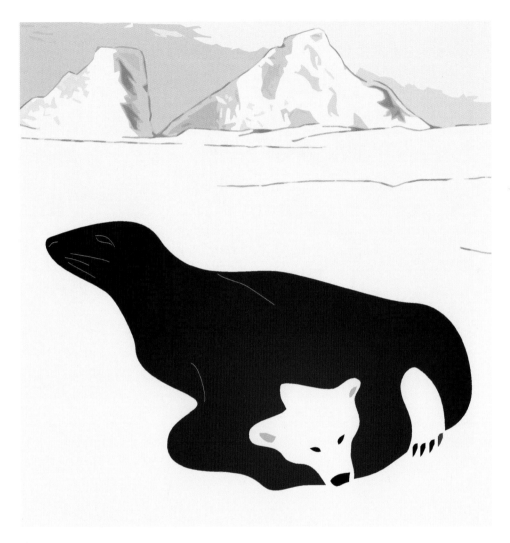

Is this a Polar Bear or a Seal?
Both, actually! A polar bear crawling out of a hole in the ice and a seal lying on the ice facing to the left.

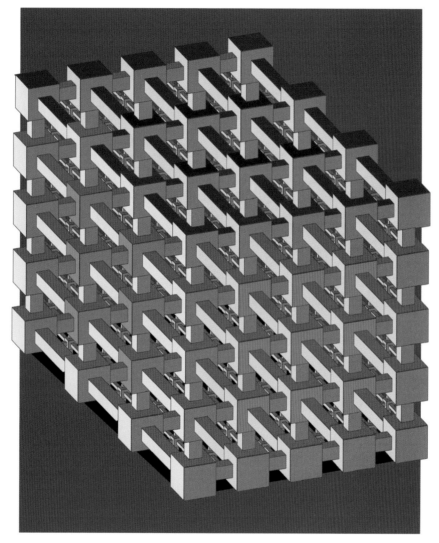

Peculiar cubic network
Actually, the network does not really represent the faces of a cube.

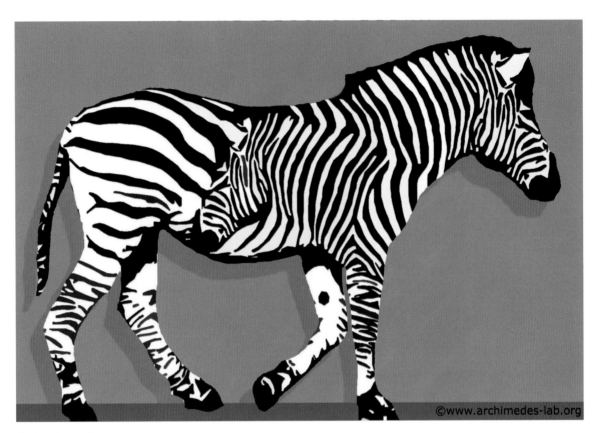

©www.archimedes-lab.org

Animal magic
Can you find a second zebra?

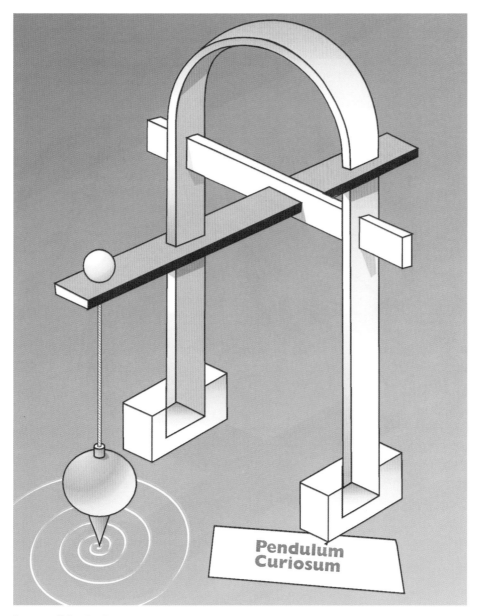

Impossible device

Just the incredible invention of a mad scientist... The feet of the
object cannot exist in our 3D world, as well as the intersecting of the boards.

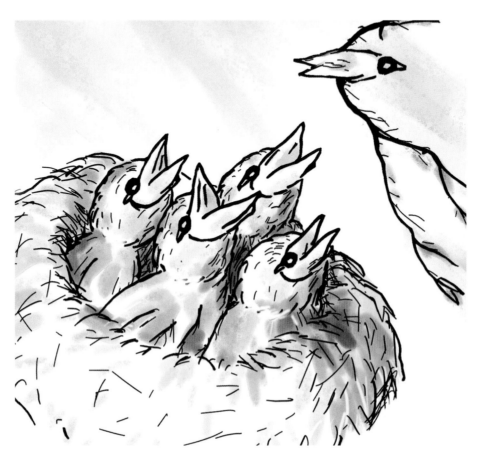

Additional birds
Can you find ten birds within the picture?

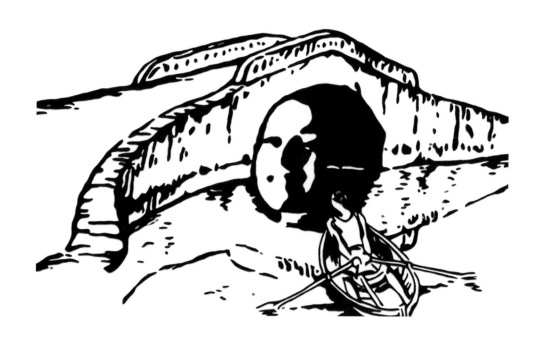

The waiting
Is the rower being watched?

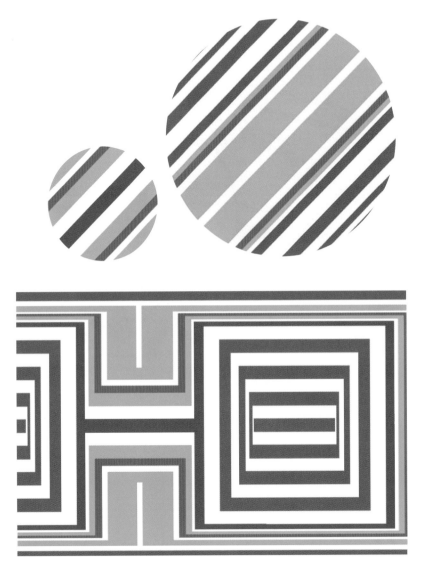

Impossible hidden discs
Can you find the two discs in the picture?

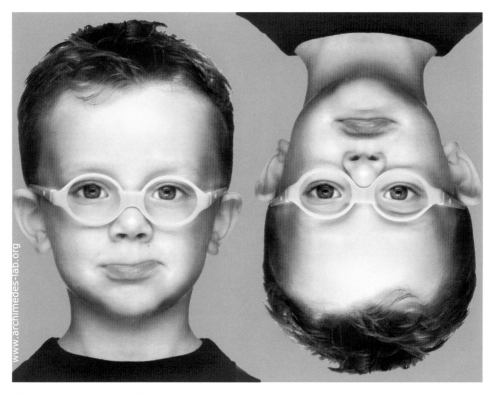

Anthropomorphic differences

Find two big differences between the boys. If you can't, turn the picture upside-down. Eek!

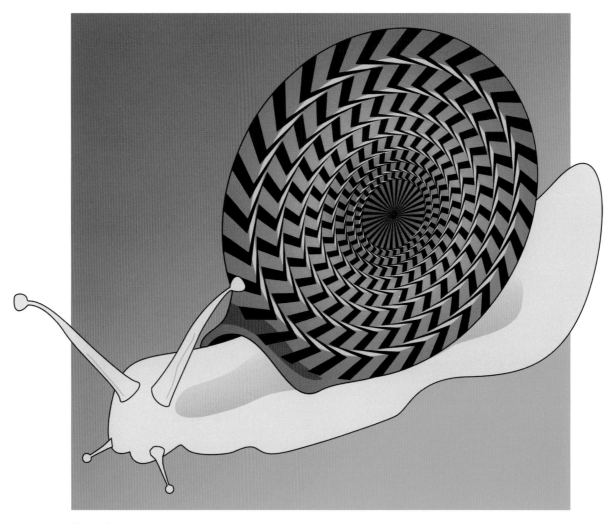

No spirals

The pattern on the snail shell is made up of concentric circles.

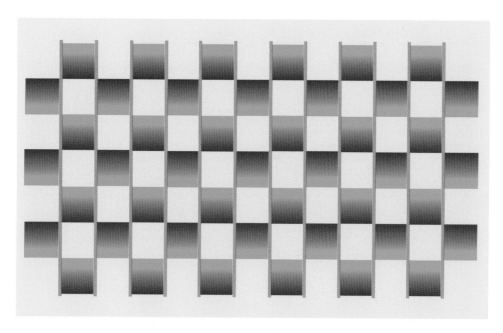

Diverging lines?

Are the vertical red lines straight and parallel to each other?

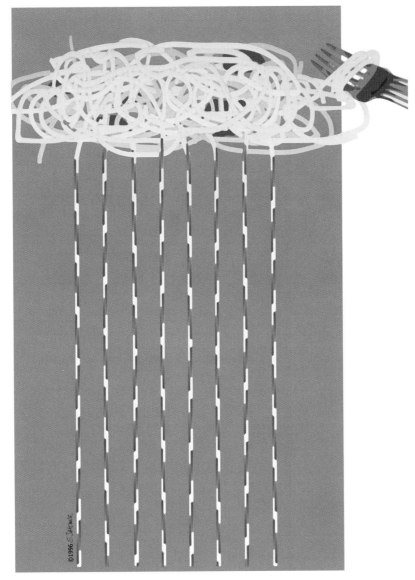

Spaghetti illusion
Does the vertical spaghetti bulge inward or outward?
Either way, buon appetito!

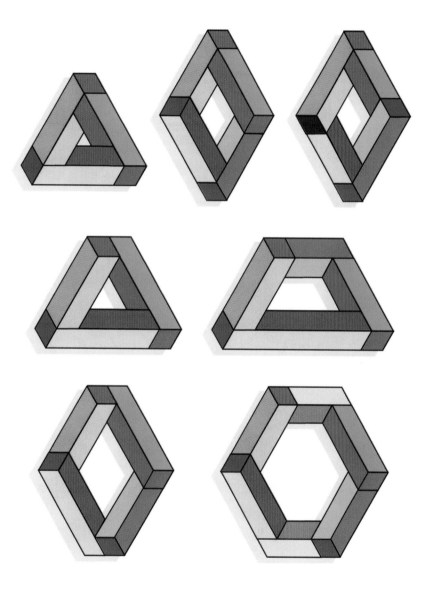

Impossible rod figures

If you want to keep children busy for a very long time, ask them to
make these figures with Cuisenaire rods.

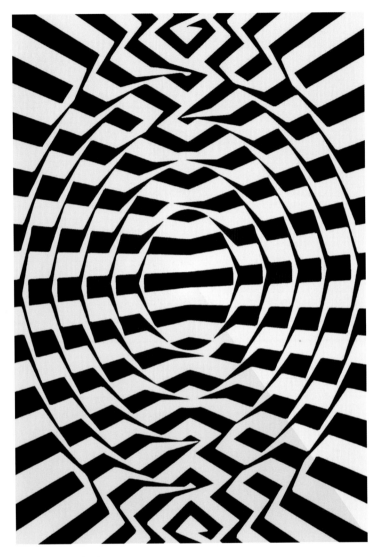

Phantom circles
The illusion of concentric ellipses is created by the connections
between the black strokes.

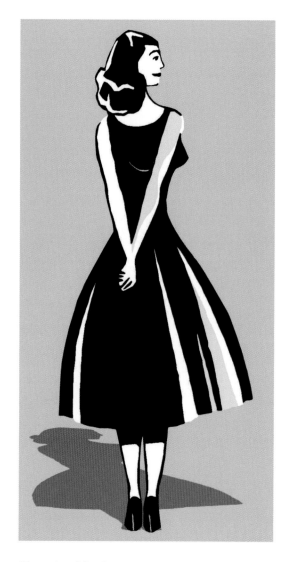

Female ubiquity
Are you looking at this woman from behind or face on?

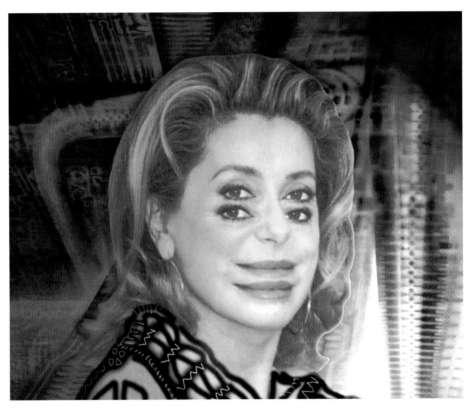

Alien vision
If you glance at the woman out of the corner of your eye, you probably won't notice her double imaging.

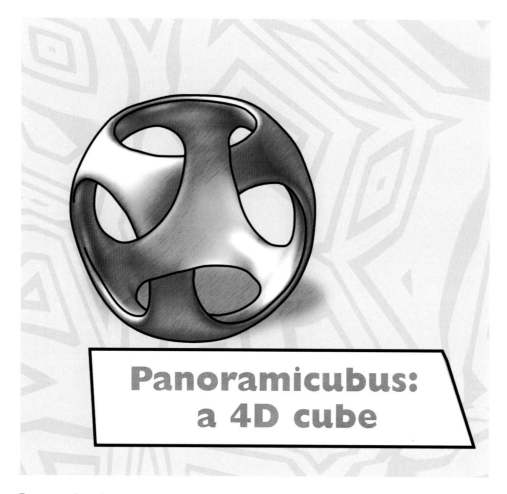

Panoramic cube
The inside of the cube is outside, and vice versa.

Gallery II Notes

Page 48

The photograph of the cow will now appear uniform. This illusion is based on color adaptation ability which allows the human visual system to compensate for changes in the prevailing color of the viewing environment. When you stare at the blue and yellow diagram, you desensitize your eyes to these colors. So, when you look at the cow again, the difference between the bluish and yellowish zones will be resorbed briefly, giving the viewer a color-balanced image – until the effect wears off.

Page 49

This is a variant of the Lingelbach grid illusion. When focusing attention on a single white dot, dark gray dots seems to appear nearby and dark brown dots a little further away. Curiously, the scintillating effect seems to be reduced when the head is tilted at a 45-degree angle. If the image is too close to your eyes or too far away, the phantom black dots do not appear.

Page 51

Two different pairs of angels!

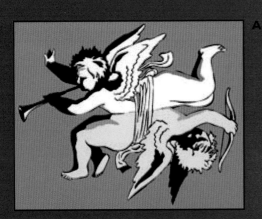

A

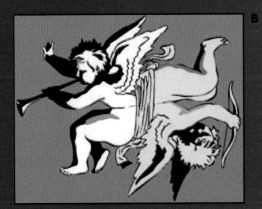

B

Page 54

It is hidden in the stripes within the breast and stomach of the zebra.

Page 56

The picture can be ambiguous: you can see either four birds sitting in four nests and one standing on a branch, or four baby chicks and mother bird (to perceive the latter, view the image from a greater distance). In all, there are ten birds!

Page 57

You can detect the face of a young woman hidden under the bridge.

Page 58

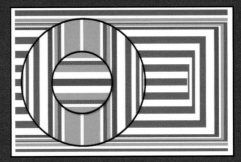

Page 59

When the face of the second boy is seen right-side-up it appears quite monstrous because he has his mouth and eyes inverted. Strangely, he doesn't appear so weird when he's upside down; this indicates that faces change depending on the angle they are viewed from. Our brain is used to seeing faces right-side-up and it is able to detect small changes in a face, but only in relation to the position of the eyes, the mouth, and the nose. When the face is upside-down our brain encounters real difficulties in spotting and judging these relative differences.

Page 61

They are perfectly aligned and parallel, even though they appear to diverge.

Page 62

They don't bulge at all! This illusion is related to the twisted cord illusion. This kind of distortion illusion was first observed in the 19th century by carpet weavers who noticed it in their patterns. In 1894, Münsterberg, a perception scientist, described this illusion in his popular collection of illusions, *Pseudoptics*. The twisted cord effect is probably due to orientation-sensitive simple cells in the striate cerebral cortex, which interact to combine a set of small, closely-spaced tilted lines into one single tilted line.

Page 65
You can see her from behind, or if you hide the shaded arm with a pencil (or any other oblong object), you will see her face-on.

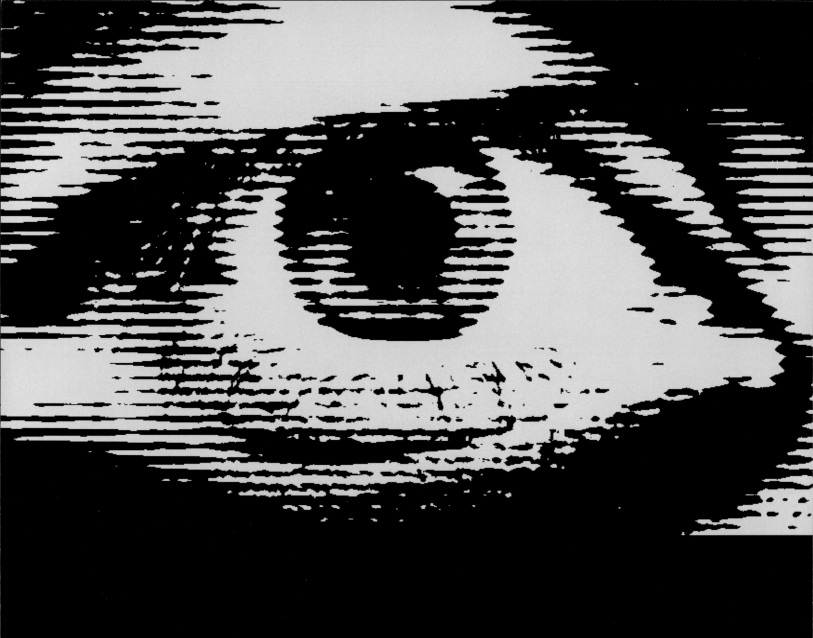

Gallery III

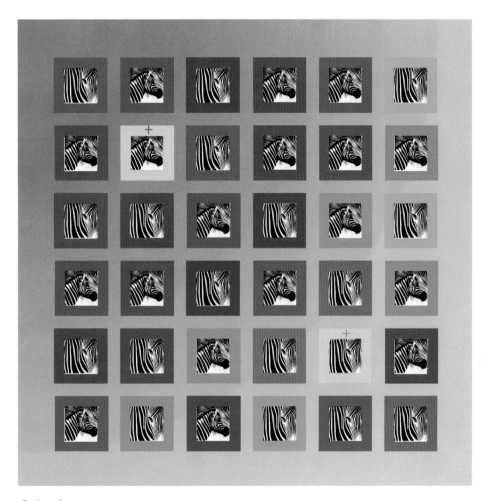

Color frames
The frames with the + sign are the same color, even though they look different. This is to illustrate that the same color affects us differently, depending on the adjacent colors. This visual effect is called simultaneous color contrast.

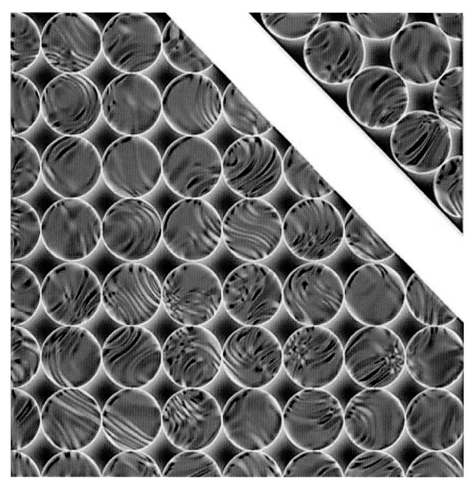

Zoltan's handkerchief

Zoltan is a magician and his favorite trick is to magically mend a torn handkerchief (as shown in the picture) by respecting perfectly its pattern; when he performs the trick all the printed discs of the mended handkerchief coincide with each other. Try to imitate Zoltan: reproduce the torn handkerchief, and cut it into five pieces, so that when the pieces are assembled they form a perfect square with 41 entire printed discs.

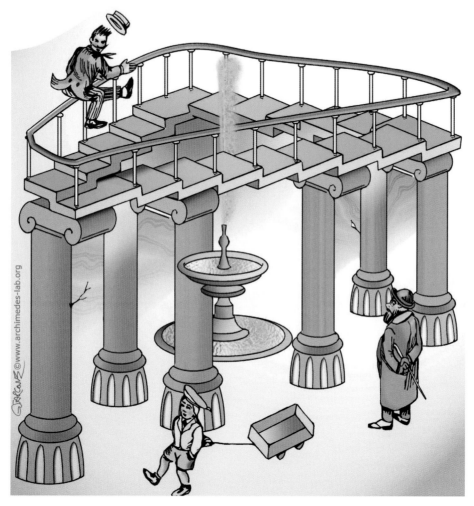

Souvenirs of Utopialand

Can you find the five oddities in the picture?

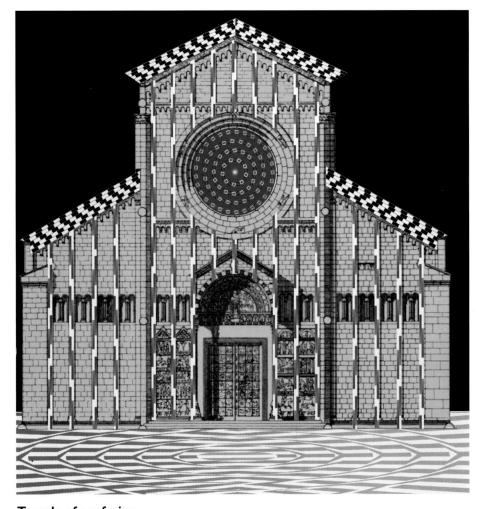

Temple of confusion
All the tiles of the temple are obviously parallel and the circles in
the rosette perfectly concentric.

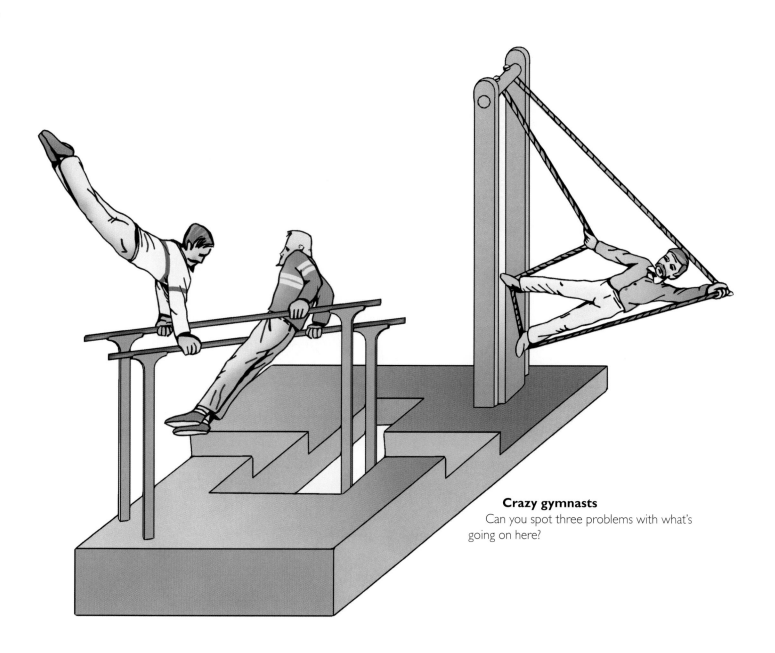

Crazy gymnasts
Can you spot three problems with what's going on here?

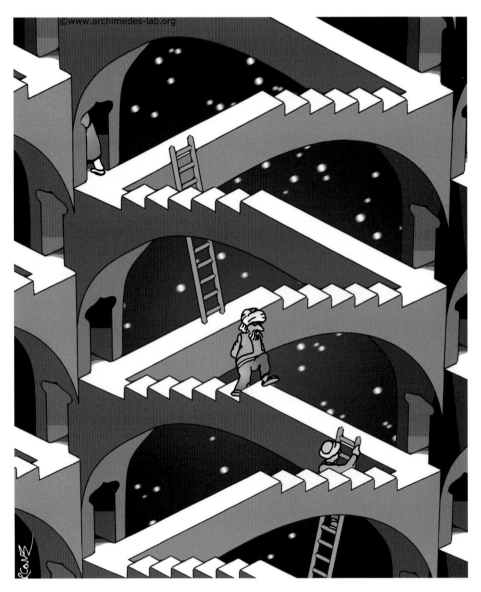

Going up?
Could you get to the top of these stairs?

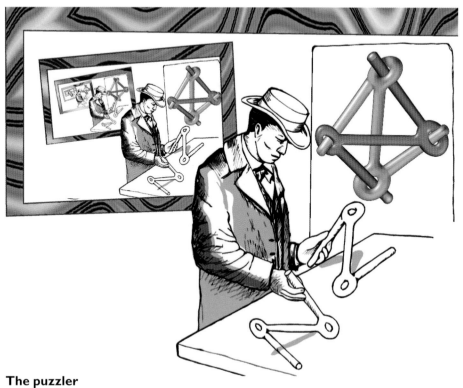

The puzzler
Can the tridimensional two-piece puzzle
shown on the poster be completed? (Notice
the special self-referential mirror...)

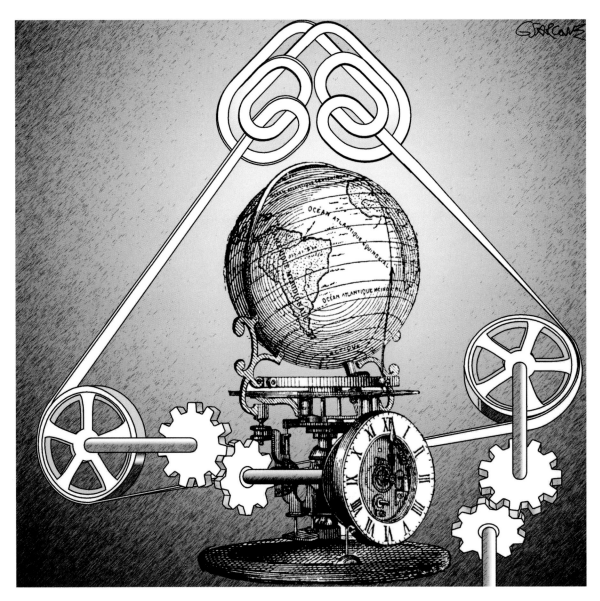

Pretzel of time

Can you spot three real impossible objects in this scene?

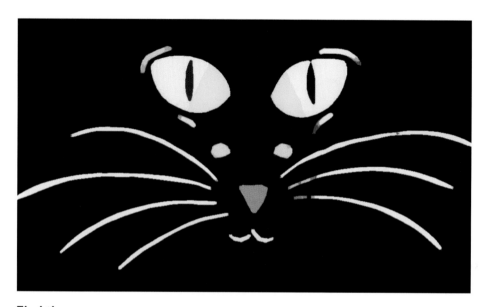

Find the mouse...
The cat is looking for the mouse. Where is it?

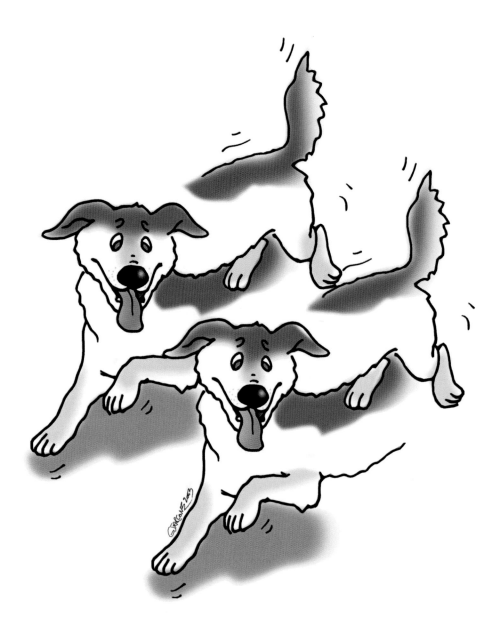

Bizarre dogs
How many dogs can you count?

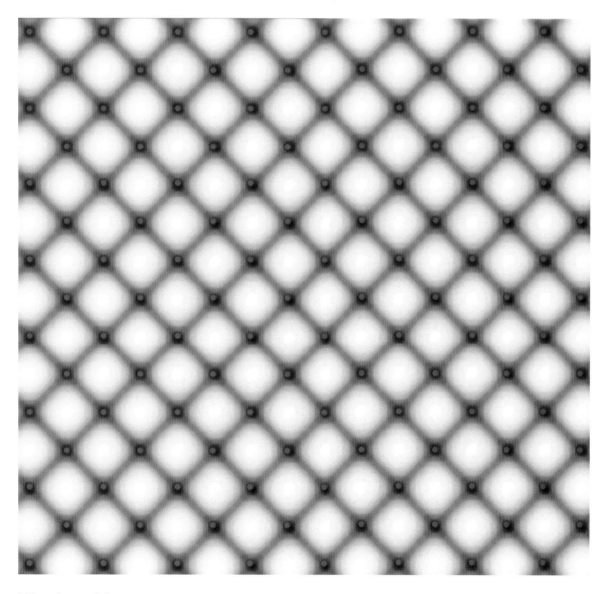

Vibrating red dots
Wow! Can your eyes bear these apparent red flashes?

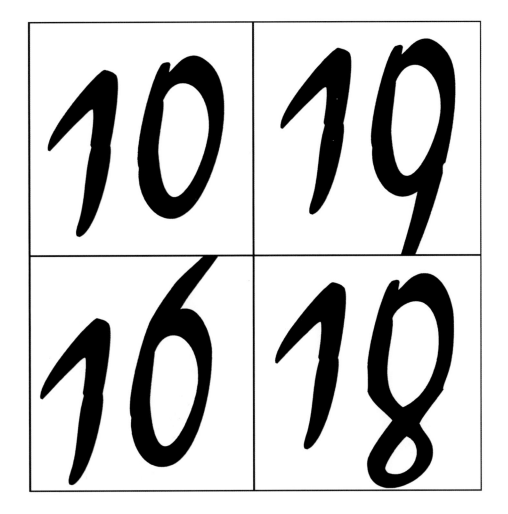

Magic 10

This trick relies on visual perception. Reproduce the picture on a cardboard sheet and cut out the four cards, each one containing a different number (10, 16, 18, and 19). Show the cards to a friend, then assemble and turn the cards over. Tell your friend that you have the mysterious ability to attract the number 10, and ask him or her to shuffle the deck and give you a card face down. Now show your card. Lo and behold, it represents the number 10! Can you guess how the trick works?

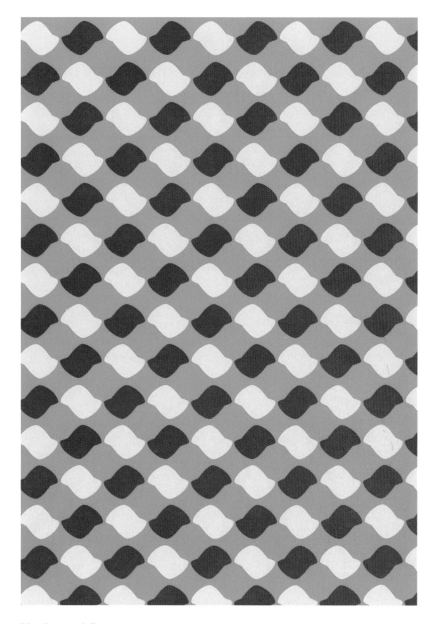

Horizontal flows
You may see flashing horizontal flows in this pattern.

Roman floor mosaic

This is a copy of the oldest apparent moving pattern. The radiating pattern of tiered plumes seems to rotate slightly.

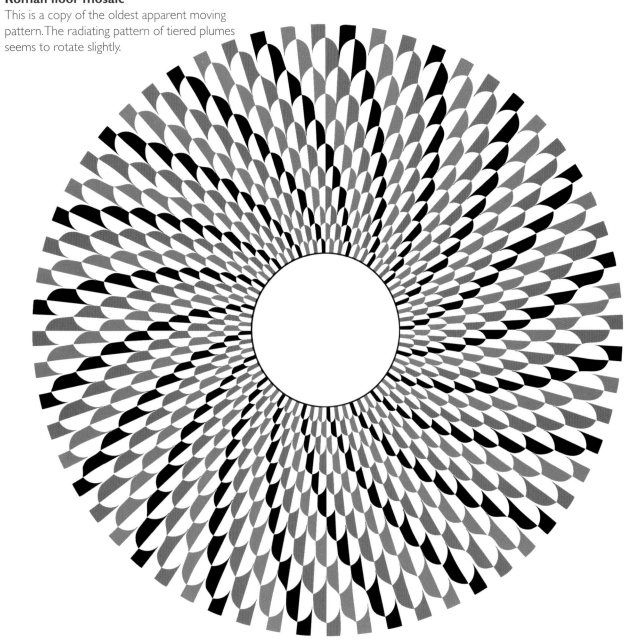

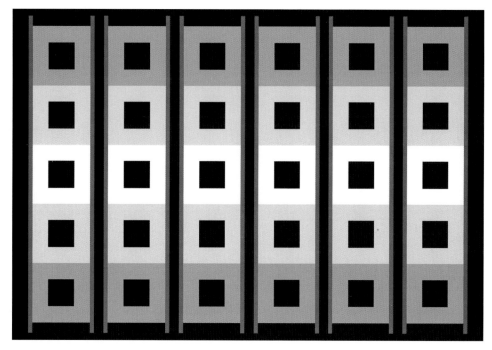

Bulging lines
The red lines appear to bulge slightly.

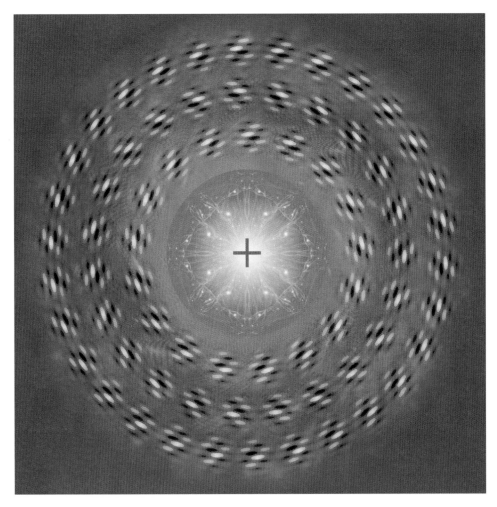

Pinna rotating effect

Some regular concentric objects appear to rotate when we approach or move back from them. Move your head backwards and forwards keeping the focus on the central cross of the image; the three circular patterns will counter-rotate!

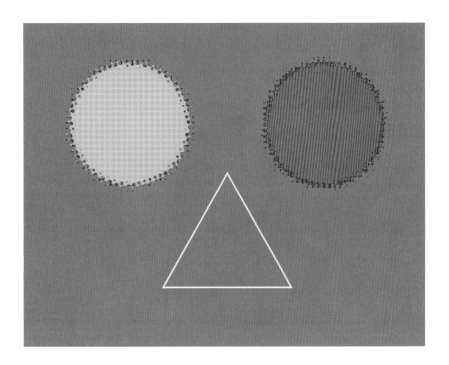

Retinal rivalry

Touch the triangle with the tip of your nose while staring at both colored discs. Now, you may see a unique disc... but can you say what color the disc is?

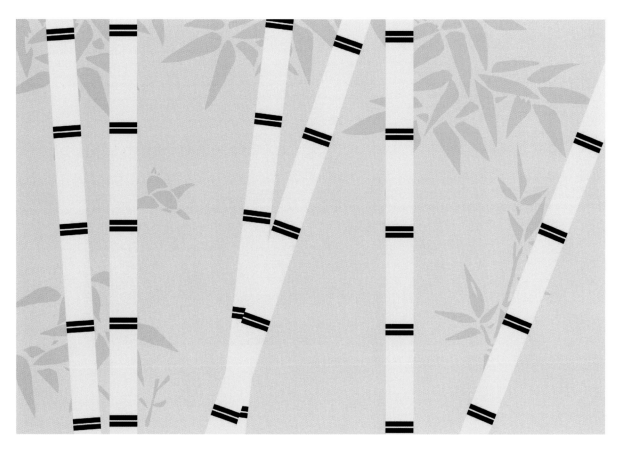

Bamboo effect
Are the yellow jointed stems of the bamboo canes really slightly
concave?

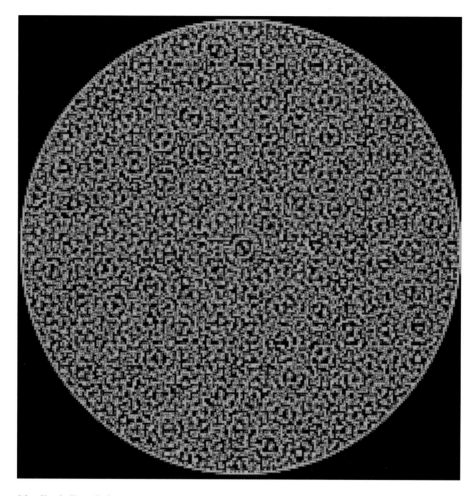

Undisciplined dots

Small circles seem to appear and disappear spontaneously as the eye moves over the disc.

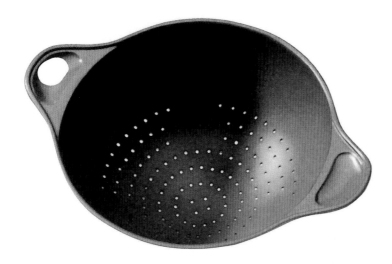

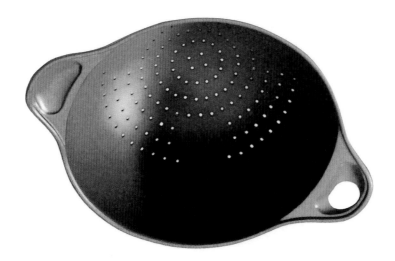

Concave or convex colander?
Depending on your point of view, the same object may appear concave or convex, as shown in the illustration.

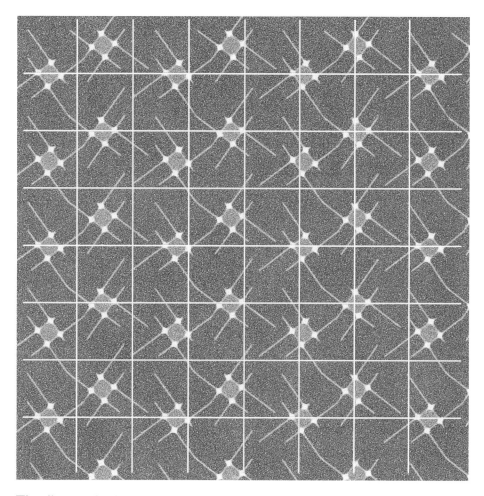

The distorted grid
Does the grid appear slightly distorted?

Gallery III Notes

Page 72

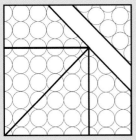 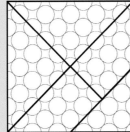

Page 73

1 The columns seem to be either cylindrical or parallelepipedic;
2 The cart of the boy has an impossible shape;
3 The upper part of the bird fountain appears in front of the column, the lower part behind;
4 The stairs appear to descend in a continuous loop;
5 The water jet passes through the banister.

Page 75

1 The two gymnasts performing on the parallel bars have two incompatible perspectives.
2 At each side of the platform can you count one or two steps? Are they perspectively ascending or descending?
3 The man who performs with the cord: does he really lean on the board to keep his balance?

Page 76

This drawing of an impossible staircase was inspired by Escher's work. Although the staircase is conceptually impossible, it does not interfere with our perception of it. Actually, the paradox is not even apparent to many people!

Page 77

No; it is an impossible figure.

Page 78

Have a closer look at:
1 The teeth of the gear wheels;
2 The belt, especially in the upper part of the drawing where it forms a kind of pretzel;
3 The axis of the wheel.

Page 79

The mouse is IN the cat. Actually, the cat and mouse share the same mouth and moustaches. The eyes of the mouse are represented by the two clear spots; the ears, by the cat's eyes.

Page 80

Don't count them. This is just a canine impossible figure!

Page 81

This scintillating effect is related to the Lingelbach grid illusion.

Page 82

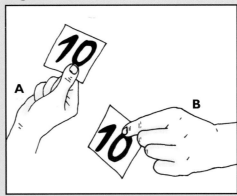

The probability is one to four that the card you receive features the number 10. If you don't happen to have a 10, but a 18 (or a 19), just hide the lower loop of the 8 (or the downstroke of the 9) with your thumb and present the card as illustrated in A. If the number on the card is 16, hide the upstroke of the number 6 with your forefinger and present the card to your friend as shown in B.

Page 83

The illusion of flows occurs when we look at certain patterns containing contrasting colors. The effect is due to the lateral inhibition of our visual system.

Page 84

The first attempt to create apparent movement with static images was done by a Roman mosaic craftsmen. This copy of a Roman floor-mosaic had in its center the head of the Medusa.

Page 85

The square patterns give the impression of bending forward along with the red lines.

Page 86

This illusion is also called the Pinna-Brelstaff rotating illusion. Bad integration of motion signals in our brain may be one of the causes of this rotation illusion.

Page 87

The two colors will not be mixed as one might think. So, the disc is 'magreenta,' alternately green and magenta because of the retinal rivalry. And if you move back slowly while staring at the test image, you may see a 'magreenta' disc floating between the two other discs.

Page 88

No; the bamboo canes are perfectly straight. Yellow color has a low spatial resolution; that means it is difficult for our brains to correctly define a determined yellow shape on a clear background. We aren't capable of seeing the vertical yellow stems as straight lines, because they tend to pull in and appear slightly curved inwards. The black inclusions enhance this concave effect.

Page 89

This visual popping-up activity is due to our visual system which is constantly searching for the best interpretation in this unorganized pattern.

Page 90

Shadows influence depth perception. We tend to assume light is coming from above; that's why when the shadow of the colander is at the top, we believe it is concave, and when the shadow is inverted, we believe it is convex.

Page 91

The grid is perfectly straight. The Japanese pattern in the background is responsible for this distortion illusion. This is a smart variant of the Zöllner lines illusion.

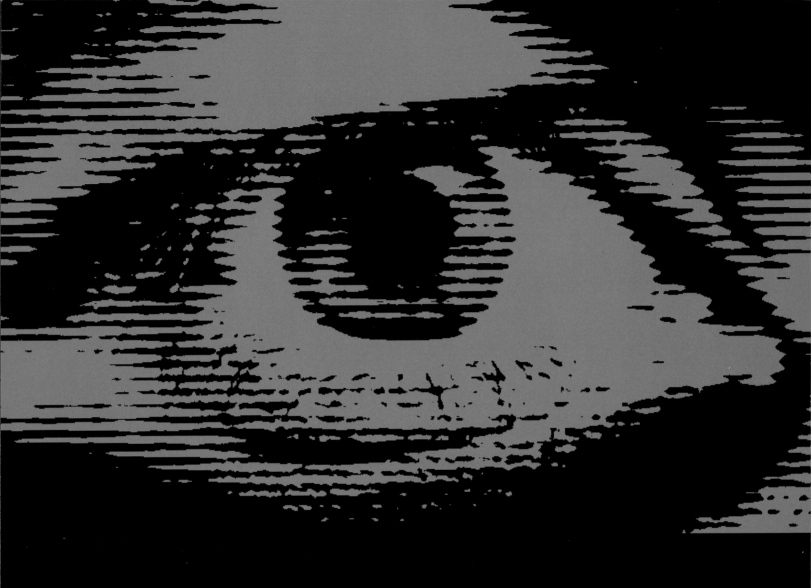

Gallery IV

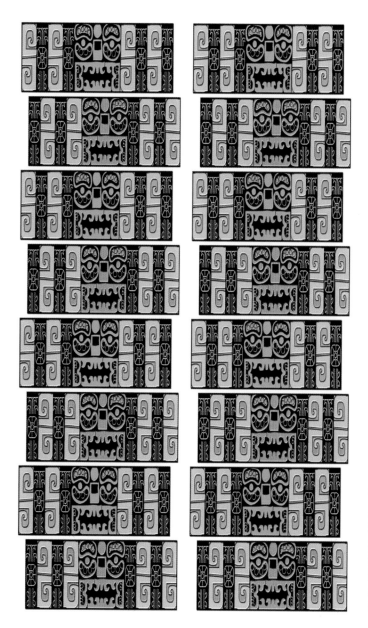

Totems

Are the stacked, rectangular figures of both totems perfectly aligned and parallel to each other? The stacked rectangular figures seem to tilt slightly, but they are parallel and aligned to each other. This illusion is related to the café wall illusion.

Rome to Paris

Ah, Paris, Paris... Are the signposts diverging at the top (where the signs are fixed)?

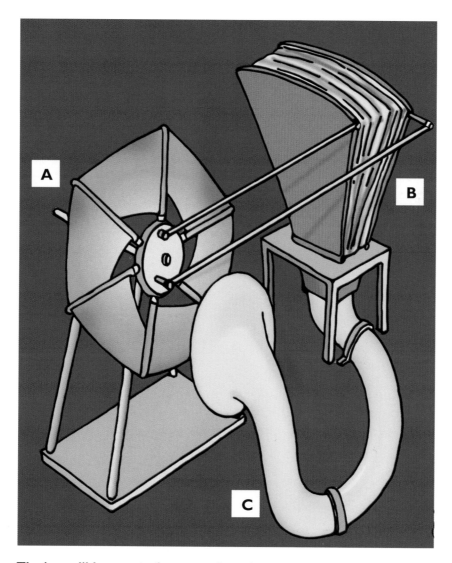

The incredible secret of perpetual motion
Turn the page over and you will discover the secret of perpetual motion.

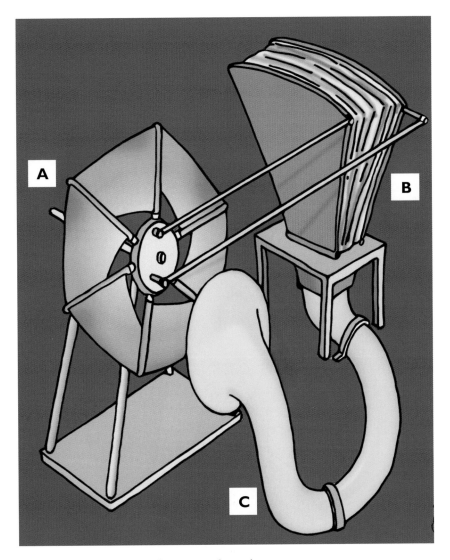

The incredible secret of perpetual motion
Flip the page back and you will discover the secret of perpetual motion.

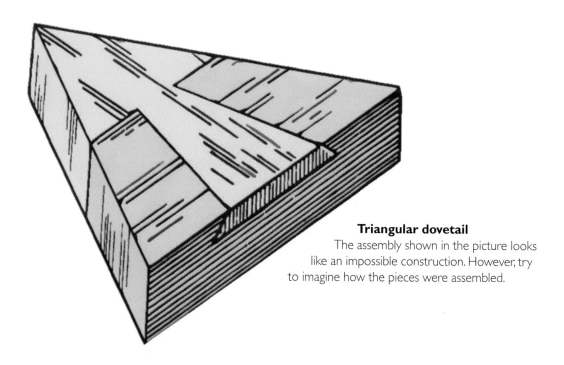

Triangular dovetail
The assembly shown in the picture looks like an impossible construction. However, try to imagine how the pieces were assembled.

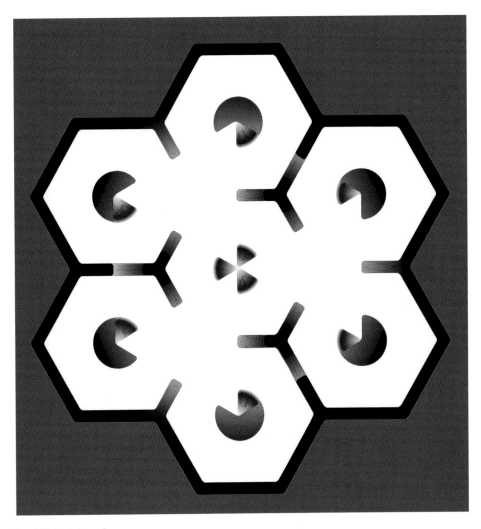

Invisible triangles
Can you perceive six triangles in this Kanisza-like figure?

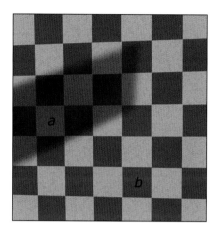

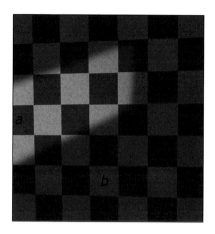

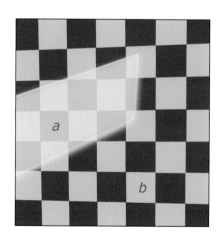

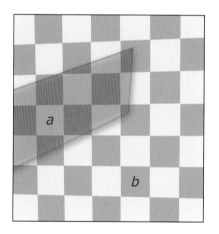

Simultaneous Brightness Contrasts

A patchwork of examples of simultaneous brightness contrasts. Every picture illustrates a particular case wherein a brightness contrast occurs. In each case, square a and square b are exactly the same shade.

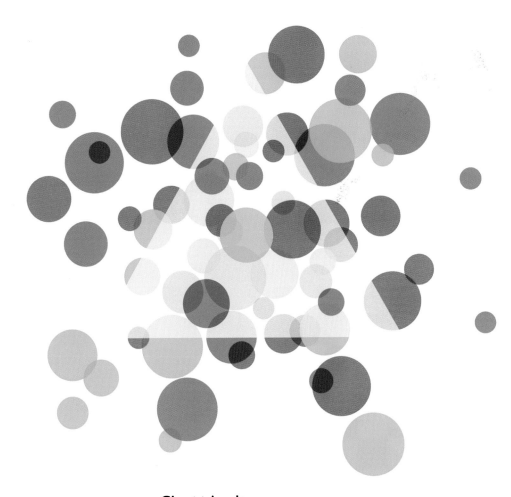

Ghost triangle

The white background looks brighter within the triangle area, but that's just an illusion. The ghostly translucent triangle actually doesn't exist at all, its outline is only determined by some colored balls!

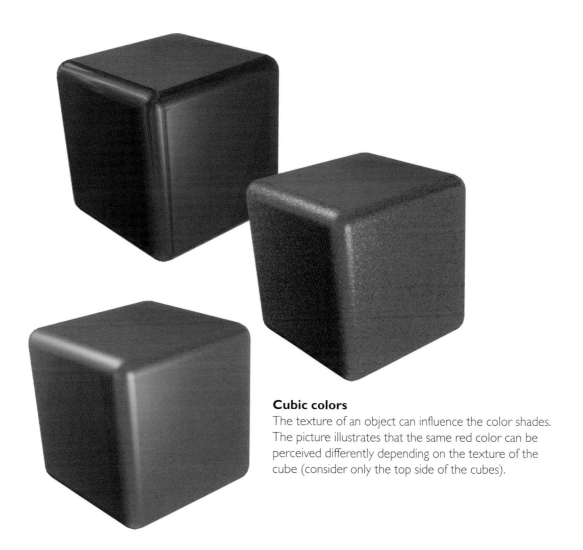

Cubic colors

The texture of an object can influence the color shades. The picture illustrates that the same red color can be perceived differently depending on the texture of the cube (consider only the top side of the cubes).

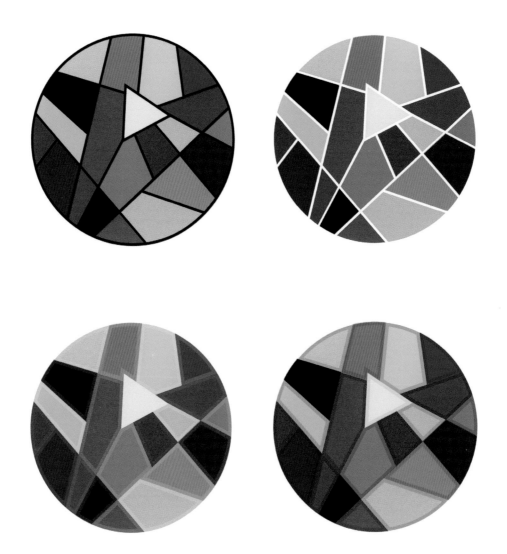

Framed colors

Frames and borderlines can subjectively modify the shade of a color patchwork. In all four examples, the colors are exactly the same; only the color (black, white) and the shade (bright, dark) of the borderlines change!

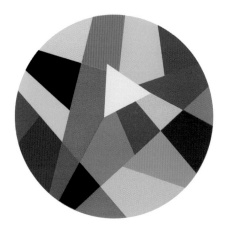
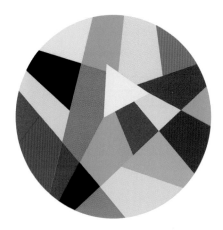

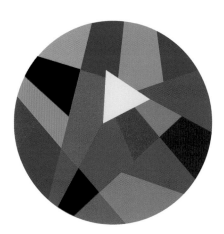
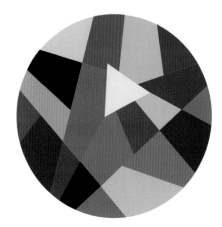

Hue induction
The yellow triangular tile is exactly the same in all four examples,
but seems to change slightly when the hues of the bordering colors are
altered. In general, a color looks most colorful against other colors in lower lightness.

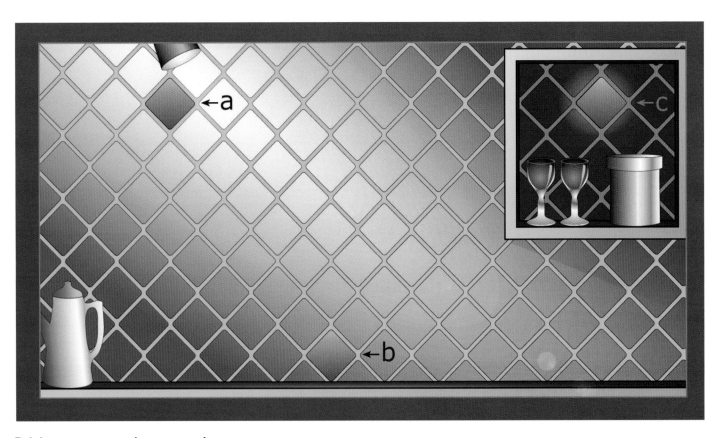

Brightness contrast in an everyday scene

The tiles a, b and c are all the same shade, despite the fact they look very different! Brightness contrast is an effect in which a color of given brightness will look darker on a light background and brighter on a dark background.

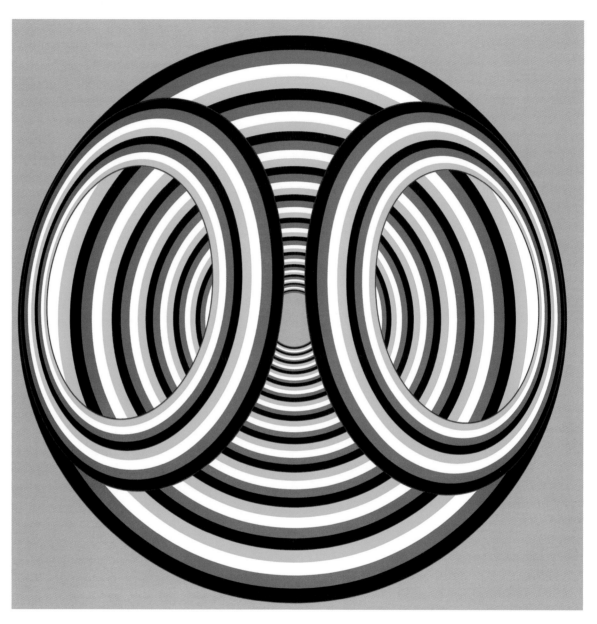

Shrinking circles

When you scan the picture with your eyes, the circles in the disc seem to shrink.

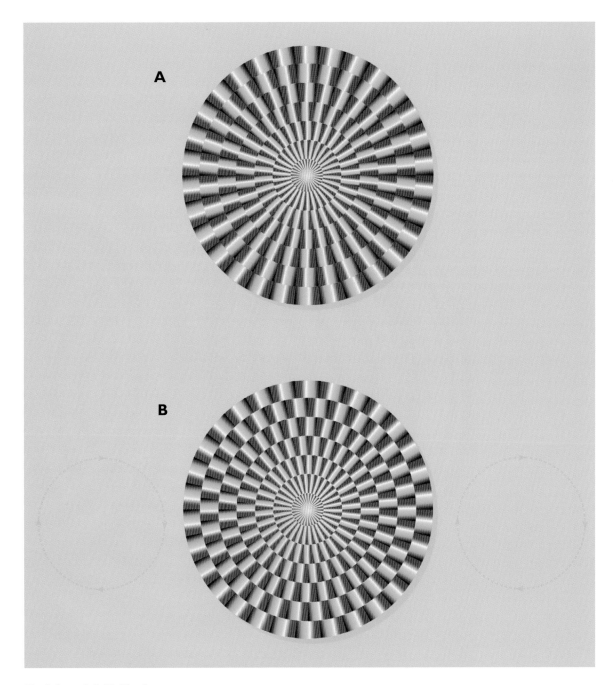

Peripheral drift illusion

Concentric repeating color patterns can induce a sensation of rotation. In figure A, however, the rotational movement is cancelled because of the conflicting luminance gradients of the concentric patterns. In B, to make the disc rotate you have to follow with your eyes the arrows placed beside the disc.

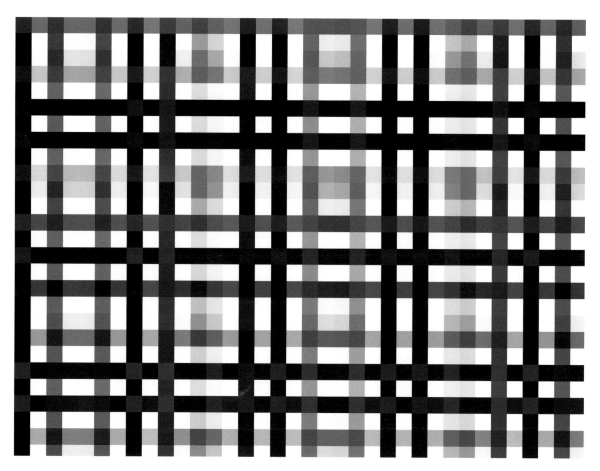

Shimmering texture

This texture seems to shimmer, especially within the intersections of the dark blue bands.

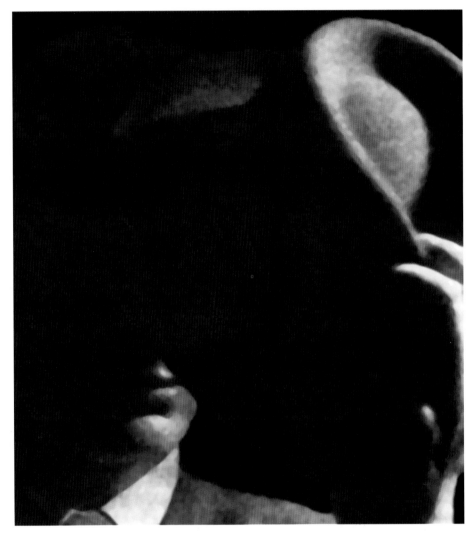

Perceptual set
"Perceptual set" is a predisposition to perceive something in relation to prior perceptual experiences. Thanks to our prior perception experiences, we can see in the picture...

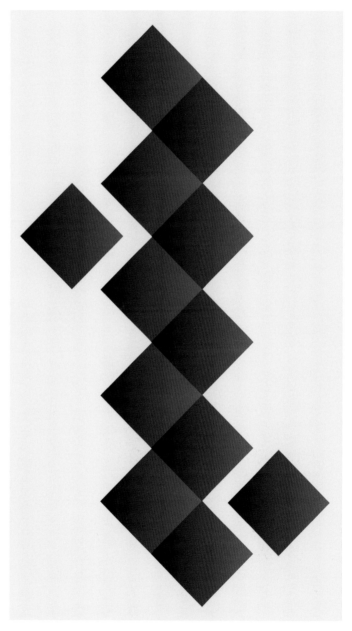

Uniform red?

Are all the tessellated red squares the same shade?

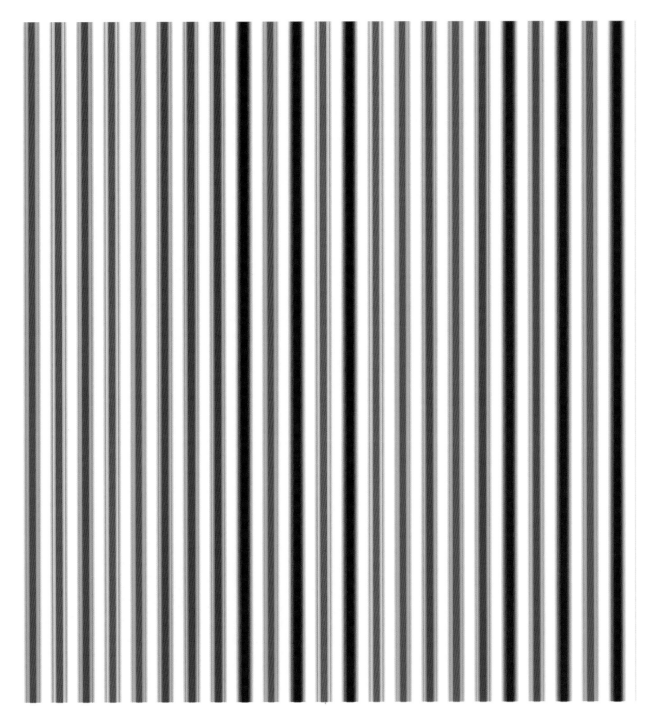

Vibrating colors

These color pipes seem to vibrate and move spontaneously. Now move your
head backwards and forwards, keeping the focus on the center of the
image; the pipes will dramatically expand and become bold! (The effect is even more
apparent on a PC screen.)

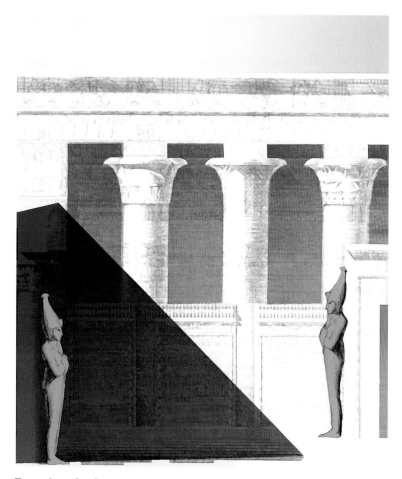

Egyptian shades

Which statue of the Pharaoh seems darker?

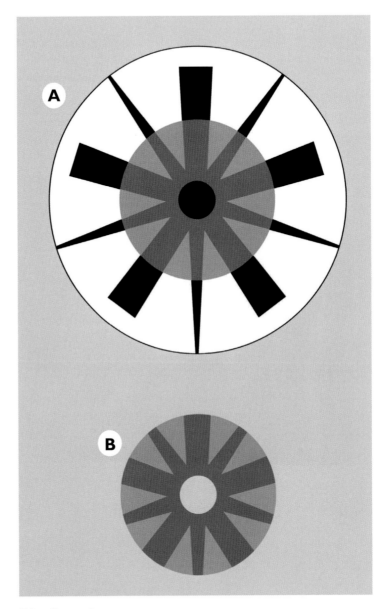

Blending colors

Both gray discs in A and B are similar. However, the shades in gray disc in A appear to blend together and to be less contrasted than disc B. The shades in disc B seem flat.

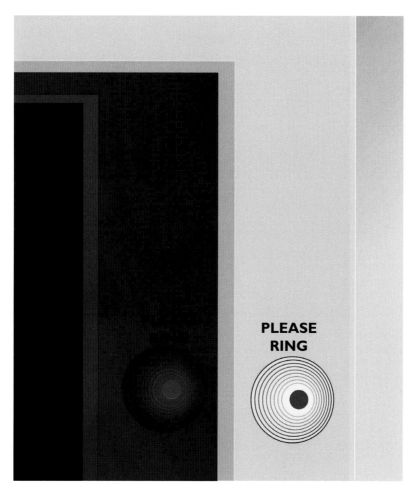

You rang?
Which button seems darker?

Gallery IV Notes

Page 96
No, they are perfectly parallel!. Take a ruler and verify them. This is another version of the twisted cords illusion.

Pages 97-98
Pages 97 and 98 are examples of a perfect self-referential joke. Self-referential sentences are a kind of verbal illusion

Page 99

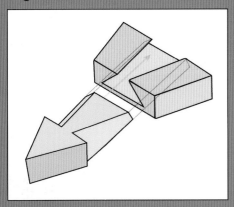

Page 102
This closure illusion is a variation of the well-known Kanisza triangle. The entire translucent triangle that covers some colored balls is created by our visual system. The effect is also called subjective or illusory contours.

Page 107
This kind of apparently self-moving shape is related to peripheral drift illusion.

Page 109
This effect is similar to the Herman grid illusion and is due to lateral inhibition.

Page 110
A man with a hat, even though the picture is mostly dark and incomplete.

Page 111
Yes, they are the same shade. Although each individual red square possesses the identical shade (left and right), when combined in a tessellated pattern (middle), the second alignment of squares is always perceived as darker than the first alignment of squares. This illusion is related to the Anstis and Watanabe diamond illusion.

Page 112
The vibrating flows are mainly due to lateral inhibition.

Page 113
They are exactly the same color. It is a "simultaneous brightness contrast" effect. Simultaneous brightness contrast is defined as the same surface appearing different depending upon the surroundings. Here the same gray target—the Egyptian statue—looks brighter in a darker surround than it does in a lighter one. This effect is mainly due to lateral inhibition (explained earlier), and can be useful in everyday life because it emphasizes a shape in a uniform background; it makes shapes more visible.

Page 115
They are exactly the same color. It is an incredible simultaneous brightness contrast effect.

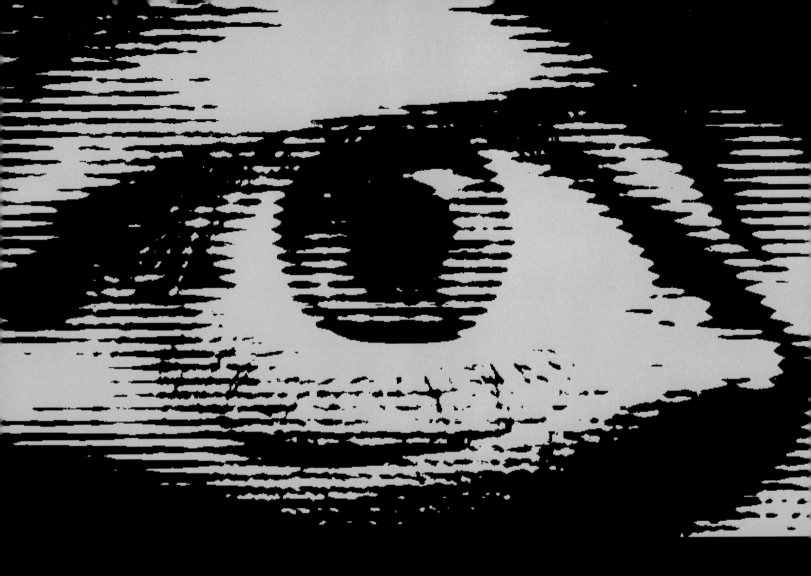

Gallery V

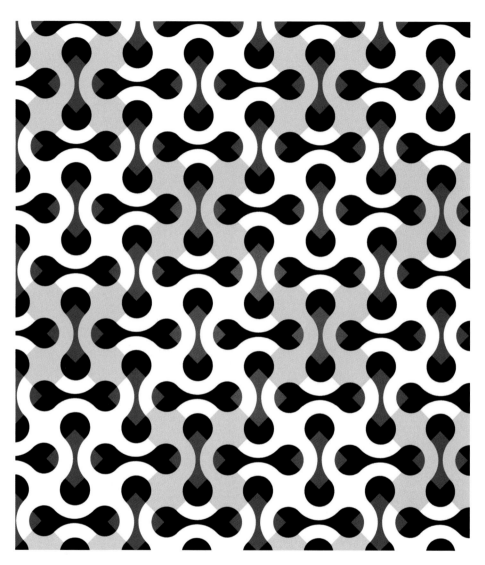

Hypnotic neon lights

Do you see a pattern of large and small squares? The apparent neon squares seem to pulse slightly when we concentrate on the image. We say apparent neon squares because the wavy pattern gives you the impression that there are whole squares lying behind it. But as the entire design lies on the same plane, the apparently pulsating squares are really just segmented colored shapes. Neon color spreading contains illusory contours, brightness induction, color assimilation, and perceptual transparency which gives depth perception. D. Varin first observed such an illusion (in 1971), but the name "neon color" came from H. Van Tuijl. The human ability to perceive a neon effect may be a remnant of the development of our power of sight under water at extreme depths, as there is a lack of light there.

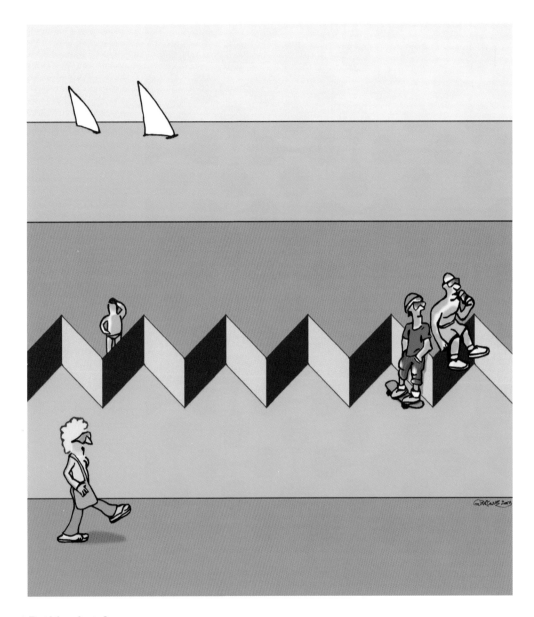

Bathing huts?
The walking woman and the skateboarder obviously aren't on the same plane...

How many triangles?

How many triangles do you perceive in the picture?

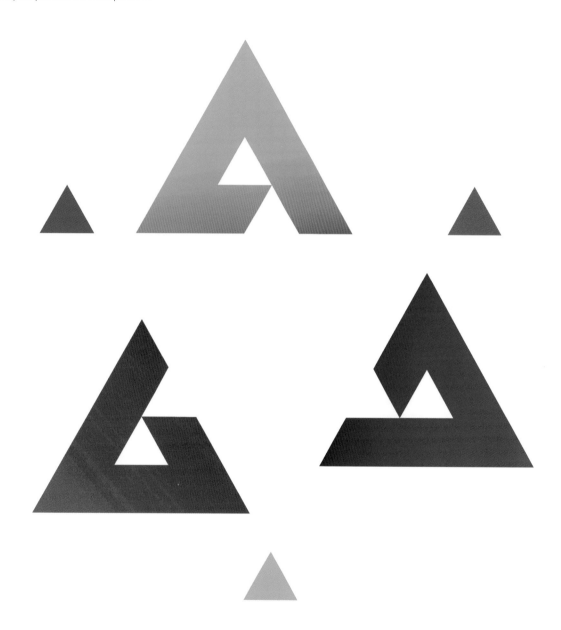

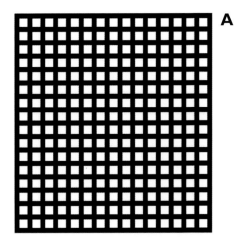

A

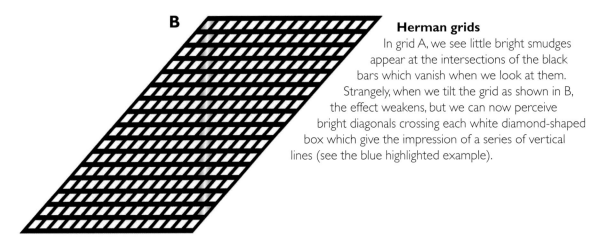

B

Herman grids

In grid A, we see little bright smudges appear at the intersections of the black bars which vanish when we look at them. Strangely, when we tilt the grid as shown in B, the effect weakens, but we can now perceive bright diagonals crossing each white diamond-shaped box which give the impression of a series of vertical lines (see the blue highlighted example).

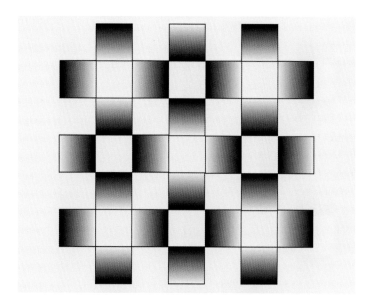

Sheen and halo effects

Using the same square composition with and without outlines, we can obtain two very different visual effects.

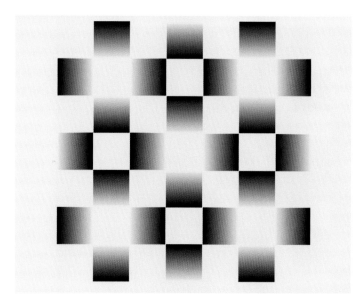

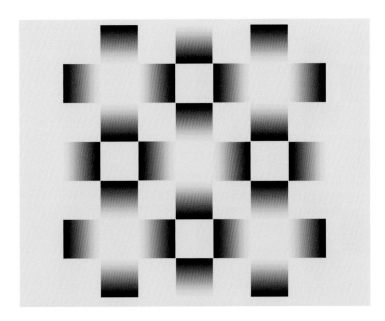

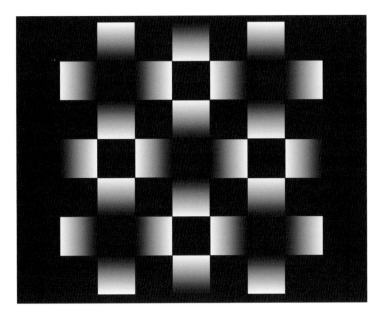

Halo and black hole effects
Using the same square composition in positive and negative, we can obtain two opposite visual effects.

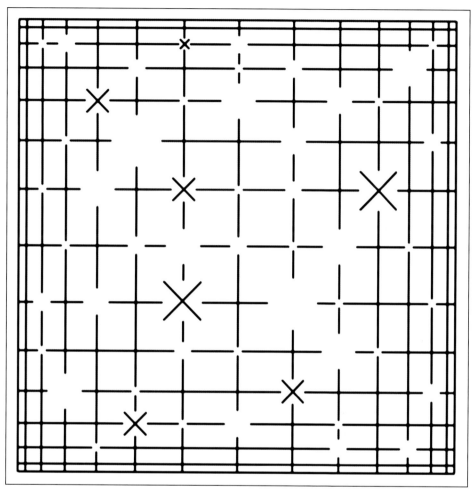

Illusory squares and spots
Can you see squares and bright spots?

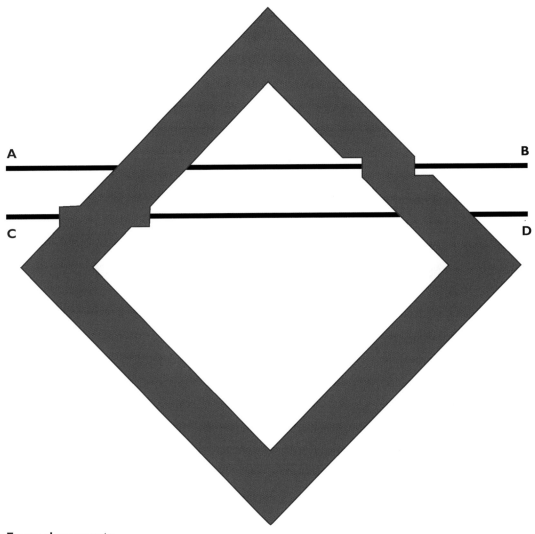

Framed segments

The two segments AB and CD go through the frame. Is segment AB perfectly straight? What about segment CD?

Light Grid

This is a variant of the "Hypnotic neon lights"; we have inverted the colors (black-blue) and this time we are able to see an apparent "neon spreading" grid. Note that the pulsating effect is absent.

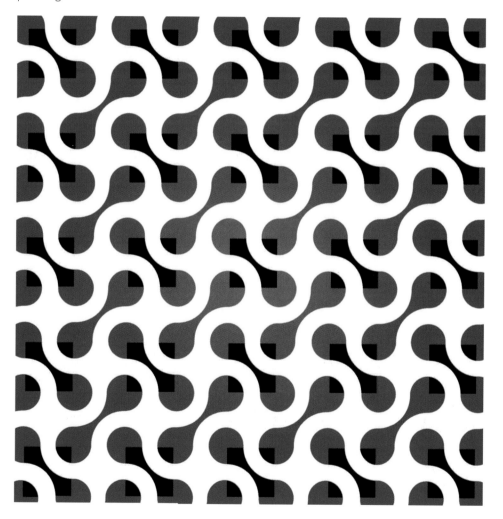

A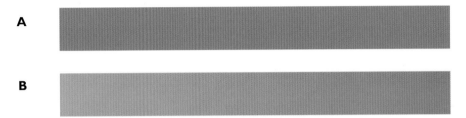

B

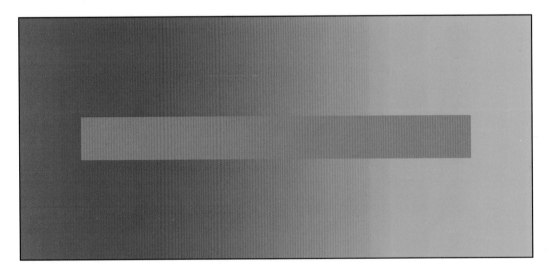

Color contrast
Which bar (A or B) corresponds to the bar
lying on the contrasted background?

A

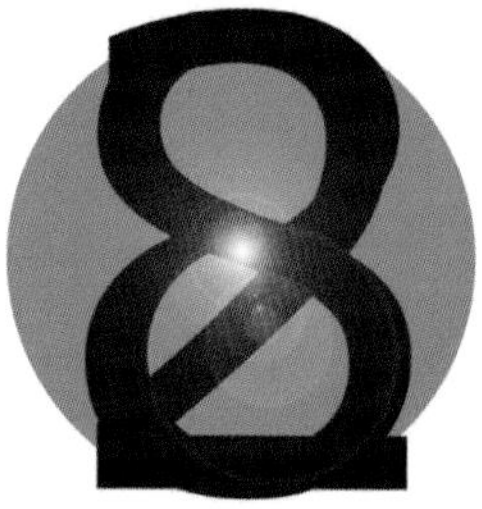

B

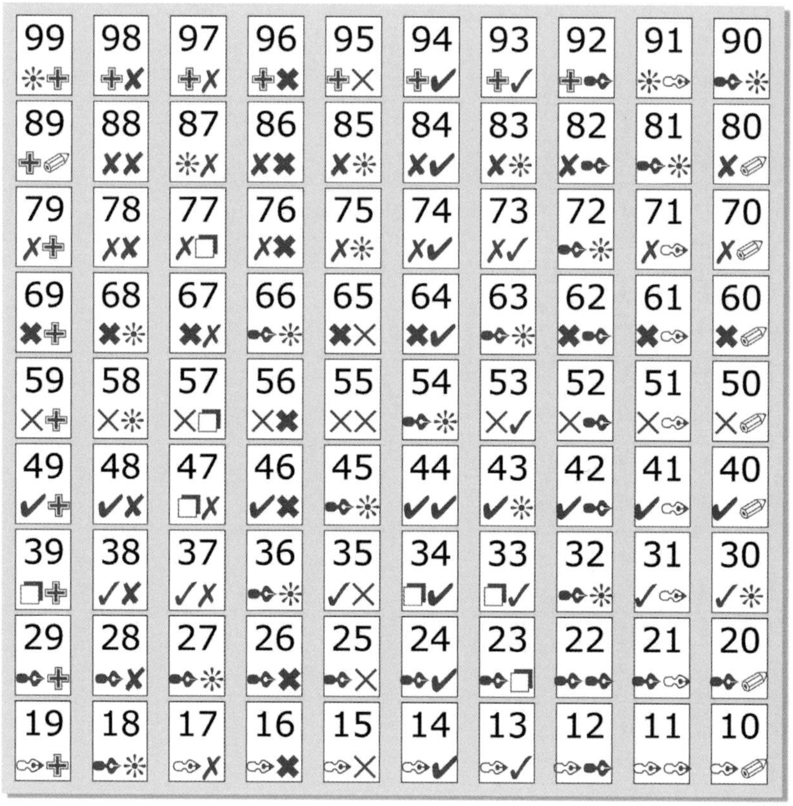

99	98	97	96	95	94	93	92	91	90
89	88	87	86	85	84	83	82	81	80
79	78	77	76	75	74	73	72	71	70
69	68	67	66	65	64	63	62	61	60
59	58	57	56	55	54	53	52	51	50
49	48	47	46	45	44	43	42	41	40
39	38	37	36	35	34	33	32	31	30
29	28	27	26	25	24	23	22	21	20
19	18	17	16	15	14	13	12	11	10

Mind reading powers

Here we will perform a magical and real mind reading trick. Follow our instructions and... relax!

Concentrate on the colored disc (A) with the strange signs inside it for 10 seconds. Now think of any number between 20 and 99 (example: 24). Add both digits together (2 + 4 = 6). Then subtract this total from your original choice (24 - 6 = 18). When you get the total, look up the number (18) on the chart to the left. Find the two corresponding symbols and focus on them.

Concentrate.

OK, turn to page 140 and you will be convinced that we are able to read your mind!

Did we get it right? Want to try again? Turn the page...

A

B

99	98	97	96	95	94	93	92	91	90
89	88	87	86	85	84	83	82	81	80
79	78	77	76	75	74	73	72	71	70
69	68	67	66	65	64	63	62	61	60
59	58	57	56	55	54	53	52	51	50
49	48	47	46	45	44	43	42	41	40
39	38	37	36	35	34	33	32	31	30
29	28	27	26	25	24	23	22	21	20
19	18	17	16	15	14	13	12	11	10

Next page!

Again, here you have to concentrate on the colored disc containing the arcane signs (A)... and think of any number between 10 and 99 (example: 72). Sum both digits together (7 + 2 = 9). Then subtract this total from your original choice (72 - 9 = 63). When you get the total, look up the number (63) on the chart on the left. Find the two corresponding symbols and focus on them. Concentrate... and turn to page 140 for the answer.

Tints and backgrounds

You can see three distinctly tinted color samples in the
picture, but when placed on the multicolored background,
the distinction seems to diminish dramatically.

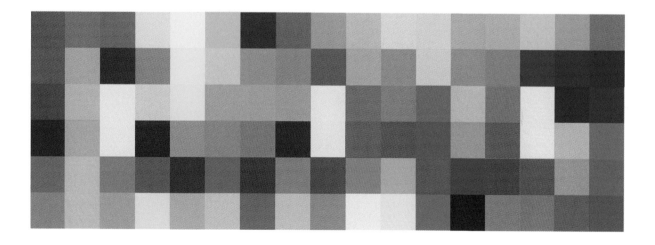

A

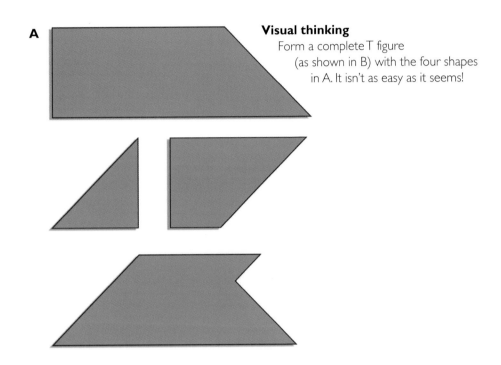

Visual thinking
Form a complete T figure
(as shown in B) with the four shapes
in A. It isn't as easy as it seems!

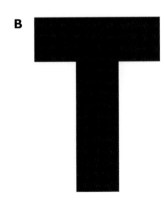

B

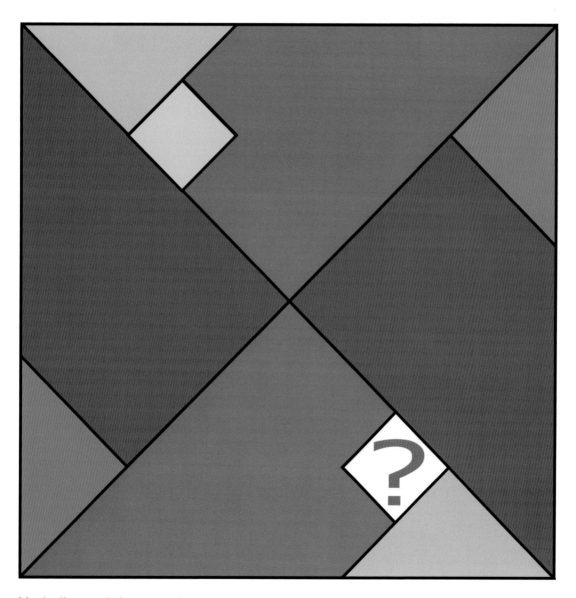

Magically mend the square!

The idea is to cut up the nine-piece color puzzle and reassemble its
pieces to form a square again — without the hole in it!

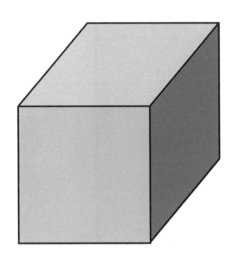

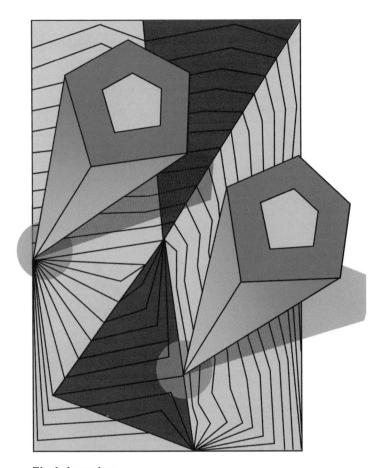

Find the prism
The outlines of the prism are
hidden in the picture...

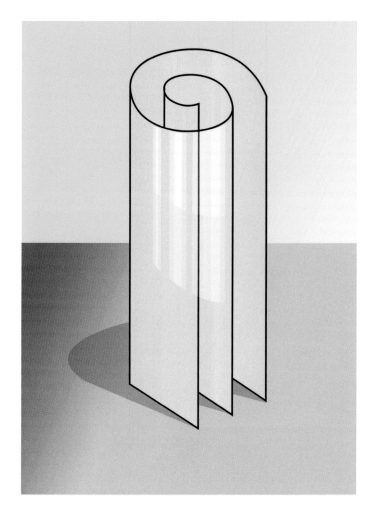

Impossible spiral
Is this a right-angled spiral?

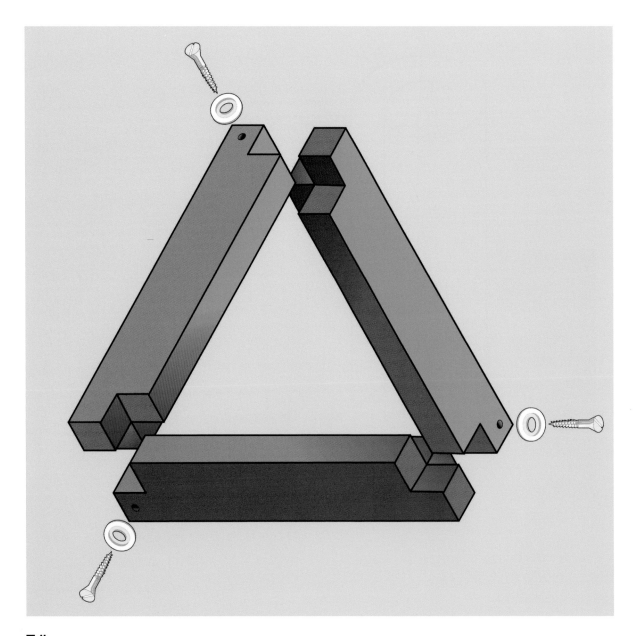

Tribar

Try to build this tribar by following the visual
instruction (take a close look at the screws
and the washers.)

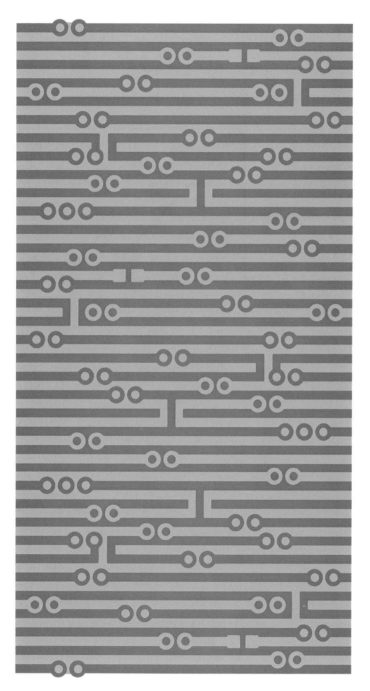

Ambiguous circuits
At a glance, you may say the background of the circuit board is blue, but are you sure?

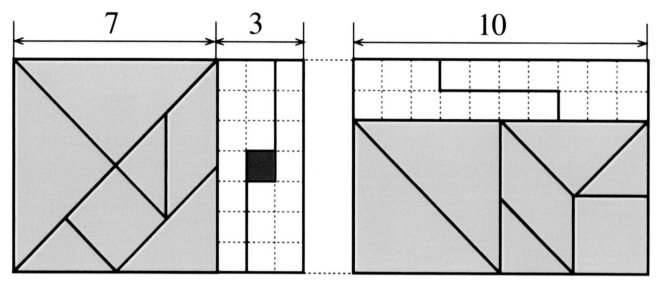

TangraMagic

This is a ten-piece puzzle. The Tangram is actually only the part in gray. With the addition of two long, L-shaped pieces and a small red square, the entire combined figure forms a rectangle. Note that the base of the rectangle is 10 units long. What is strange is that we can assemble the rectangle without the small red square and in this case, the area appears almost identical. How can you explain this?

The mischievous leprechaun

Position yourself approximately 30 centimeters in front of the diagram. Close your right eye and with the other, focus on each number one at a time. Count up at one-second intervals. By the time you get to number 4, the leprechaun may seem to have wandered off the circle.

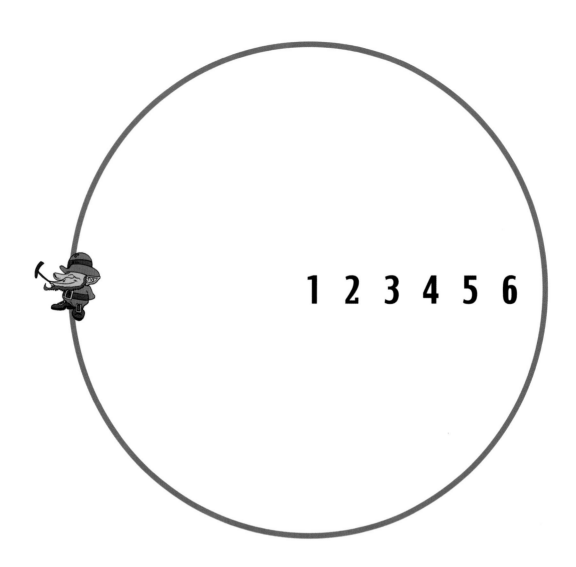

Gallery V Notes

Page 121

There are in all 11 triangles: three small white triangles, three small colored triangles, three large colored triangles, and two illusory bright triangles.

Page 122

Up until now, there are no definite answers to explain the apparition of bright smudges on the grid. One much-debated theory suggests that the contrast between the white boxes and the black spaces makes the spaces appear blacker. At the intersections there are no adjacent, contrasting white sections, so the black spaces appear a bit less black, hence the 'grayish' effect.

Page 125

On this grid you can see several Xs; the four points of each X determine an illusory square. You may also notice areas of apparent bright discs that actually don't exist. These illusions are related to the Kanisza triangle illusion. These illusory figures depend on "gaps" in the grid lines.

Page 126

Both segments are perfectly straight. Strangely, the portion of segment AB which enters from A (on the left) doesn't appear to be in alignment with the whole segment. The same applies to segment CD. The portion which enters from D (on the right) doesn't appear to be aligned with the rest.

Page 128

This illusion is based on the simultaneous color contrast effect. The green bar on the contrasted background is the same shade throughout. Therefore, the answer is bar A.

Page 129

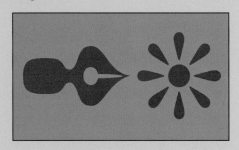

The image above shows the two symbols you thought of, right?

Page 130

We guessed right again, didn't we?

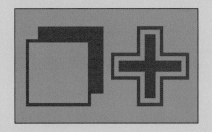

How it works

We mislead your attention using images. Yes, you concentrate on images, but the trick is based on a simple math rule. To understand this magic trick, try doing it again and again.
(Hint: why do you think the numbers you select are all multiples of 9?)

Page 131

This color experiment shows you that different tints are more difficult to distinguish on a colored background than on a uniform background.

Page 132

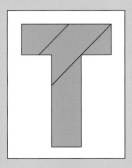

It's difficult to judge the correct position of the diagonal shape which joins the other pieces together because we tend to concentrate more readily on the horizontal and vertical aspect of the world around us than the diagonal.

Page 133

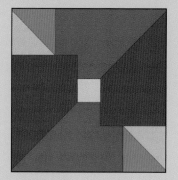

Page 134

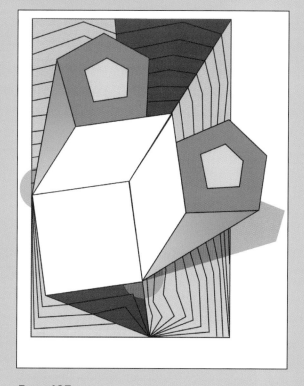

Page 137
The background is either blue or red. It's a kind of undecidable figure.

Page 138
In the second diagram, the Tangram appears to occupy 10 × 5 = 50 square units, while it is clear from the first diagram that the area of the Tangram occupies a square area of 7 × 7 = 49 square units. If the gray rectangular Tangram portion is packed tightly and measured, you will find that it is slightly less than the apparent 10 × 5 dimensions. Actually, the real area of the gray rectangle is

approximately 4.95 × 9.9 = 49. The discrepancy is equal to 50 − 49 = 1 square unit which is the area of the red square.

A short history of the Tangram... Little is known for certain about the origin of the Tangram. Even the origin of the name is obscure! The earliest known book was published around 1813 in China. A Tangram-like puzzle first appeared in a book published in Japan in 1742. Scholars assume that Tangrams originated from the Orient before the 18th century and then spread westward. In the past, the adjective "Chinese" was commonly used to denote any odd, complicated or contrived thing and not the origin of the object! By 1817, Tangram publications had appeared in the United States and in Europe. Whatever date the Tangram was invented, you have to know that rearrangement puzzle roots can be traced back to the 3rd century BC! Back in those days Archimedes, a Greek mathematican, designed a Tangram-like puzzle called *Loculus Archimedis* or *Ostomachion*.

Page 139
In our visual field there is a very large spot, called the blind spot, where the optical nerve enters the eye. This region has no photoreceptors. So, when the leprechaun enters your blind spot he naturally disappears (from view).

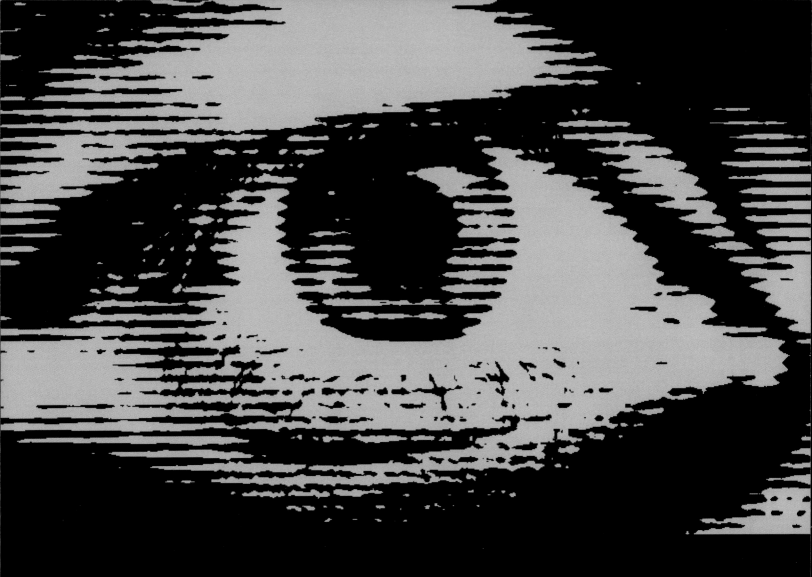

Gallery VI

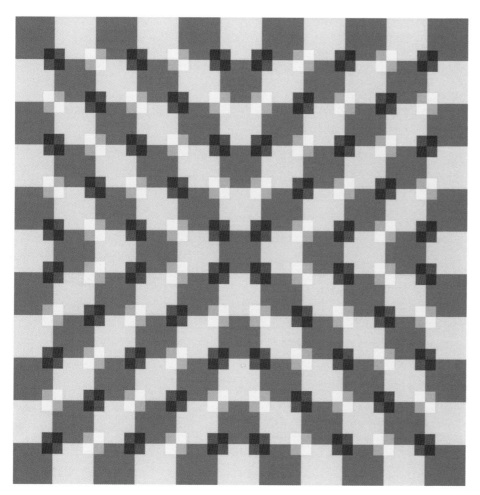

Bulging square
Is it a convex square?

The small dark and light squares on the foreground create a "subliminal" crossing pattern that constrains the alignment of squares on the background to appear slightly bulging. This illusion is related to the Zöllner illusion. You can perceive the "subliminal" crossing pattern by looking at the picture with half-closed eyes.

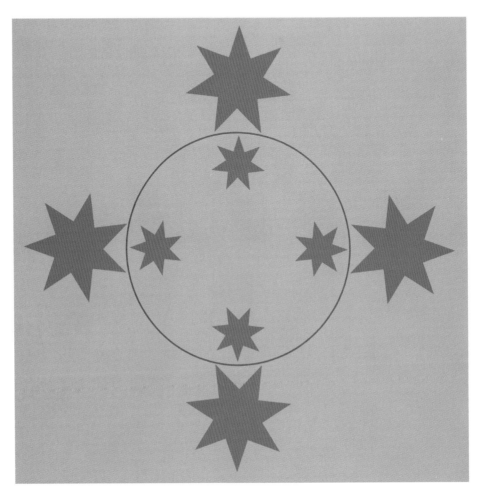

Perfect circle?
Is the red circle really 'circular?'

Fooling cross

Are segments AB and CD the same length?

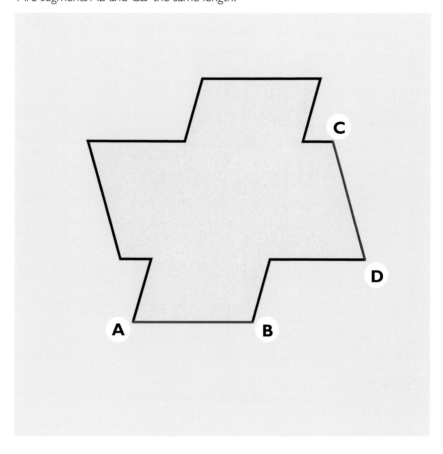

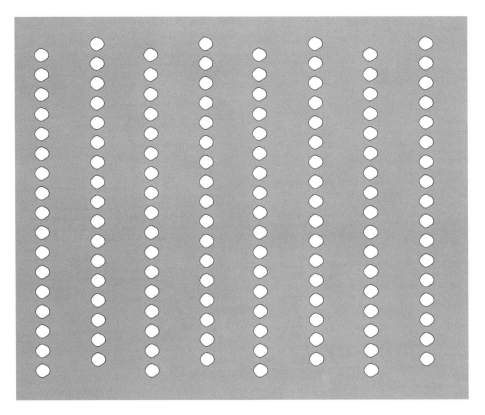

Floating flakes

Are the lines of floating flakes perfectly parallel? Do they move imperceptibly up and down?

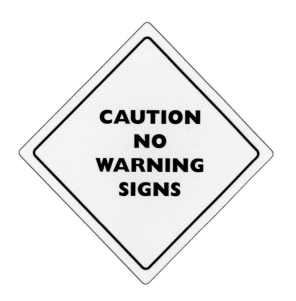

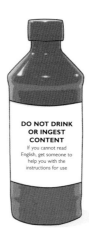

Verbal illusions

Why is the sign paradoxical? And what about the message on the bottle?

Both objects contain a paradoxical self-referential sentence.

A sentence is said to be self-referential when it refers to itself. It illustrates somewhat the relationship between meaning and the symbolism of meaning. Paradoxical self-referential sentences can confuse our minds; they are like impossible figure illusions; they exist, but are not understandable as a "whole," yet interpretable as an "oscillation" of two contrasting levels of meanings. Here are some everyday self-referential paradoxes:

– There are ALWAYS exceptions
– You're unique like ALL of us
– This species has ALWAYS been extinct
– Superstition brings bad luck
– I refuse to join a club in which they accept members like me
– Is 'NO' your answer to this question?
– Expect the unexpected (Heraclitus)
– The two rules of success are: first, never divulge everything you know
– Be spontaneous!
– Stop obeying me!

The writing in the sign means that the sign itself isn't a warning sign… But this is in contradiction to the word "caution." In the second example, how can someone who doesn't read English read the sentence 'if you cannot read English' on the label of the bottle?

Sure, not all self-referential sentences are paradoxical. Some are comparable to an "autistic" sentence which communicates with itself in loops (a sort of logical computer-type bug). The following short story illustrates the principle:

A Brief Reflection on Accuracy by Miroslav Holub (thanks to Professor Sergio Della Sala who brought this story to our attention).

A certain soldier had to fire a cannon at six o'clock sharp every evening. Being a soldier, he did so. When his accuracy was investigated he explained, "I go by the absolutely accurate chronometer in the window of the clockmaker down in the city. Every day at 1745 (5:45 p.m.) I set my watch by it and climb the hill where my cannon stands ready. At 1759 (5:59 p.m.) precisely I step up to the cannon and at 1800 (6:00 p.m.) sharp I fire."

It was clear that this method of firing was absolutely accurate. All that was left was to check that chronometer. So the clockmaker down in the city was questioned about his instrument's accuracy. "Oh," said the clockmaker, "this is one of the most accurate instruments ever. Just imagine, for years now a cannon fires at six o'clock sharp every evening and my chronometer has always been bang on the hour…"

To conclude, here are some non-paradoxical self-referential sentences:

– This sentence finishes right here
– Pentasyllabic (is a word of five syllables and means 'a word containing five syllables')
– This sentence was in the past tense
– You may quote me

The middle point
Which line (A, B or C) is positioned
exactly halfway up the spine of the book?

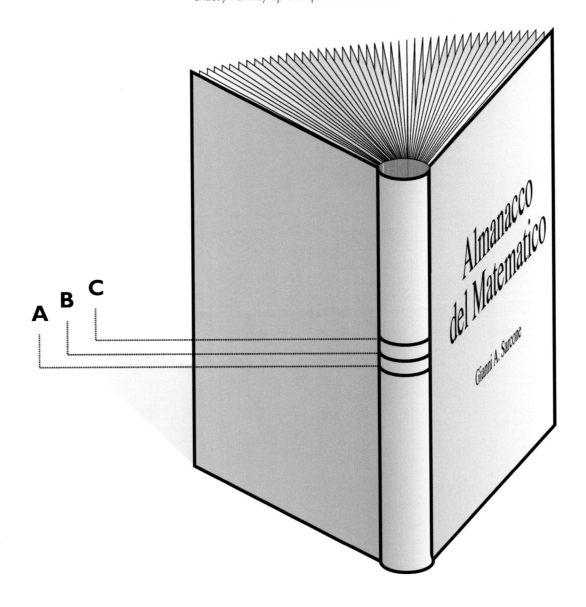

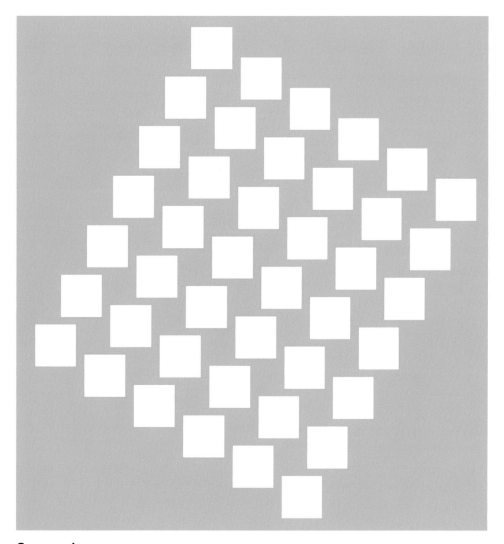

Squeezed squares

Are the white shapes perfect squares?
Do they have "pointed" corners?

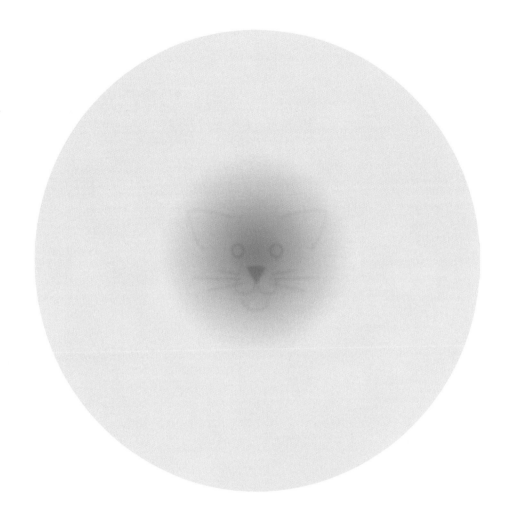

Cheshire Cat

Close one eye and focus your attention on the central blue haze to make
the Cheshire Cat vanish. You'll notice that after approximately 15-20
seconds the blue haze gradually disappears along with the cat, but if
you continue to stare, the cat will reappear...

90-degree angles
How many 90-degree angles are hidden in the picture?

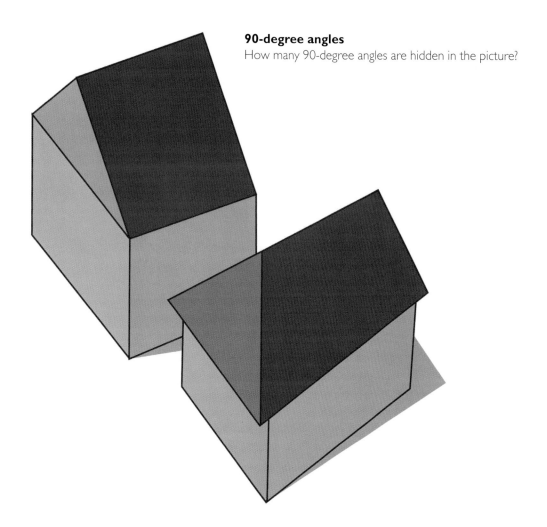

Bowling ball illusion

Which ball is larger: the one which has been dropped by the player or the other one in the foreground?

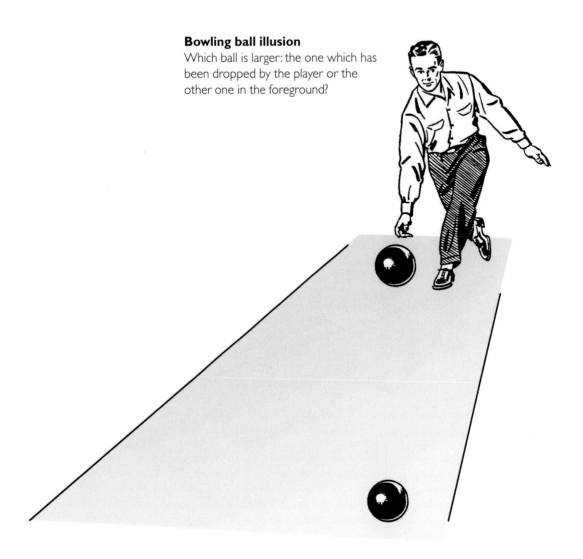

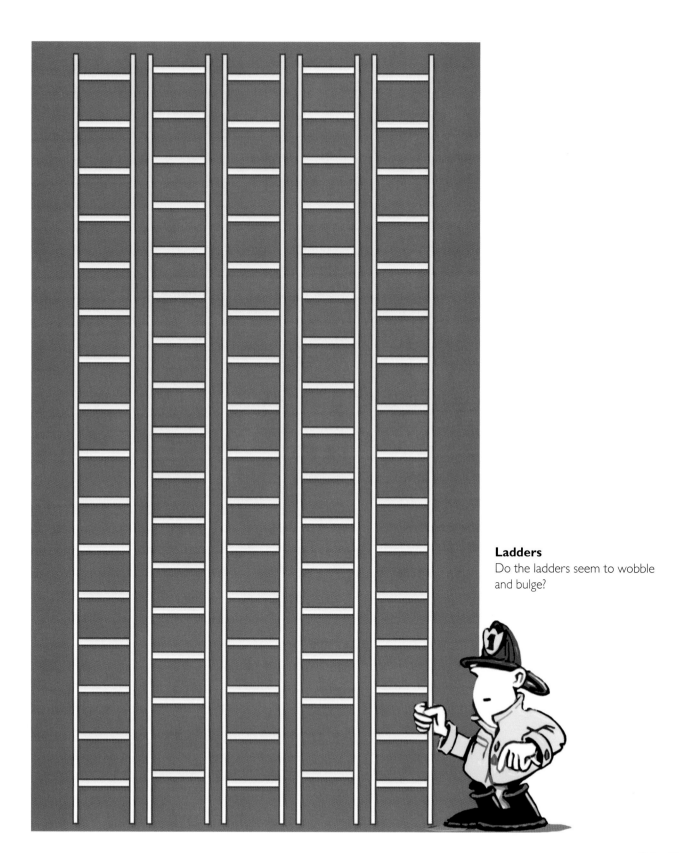

Ladders
Do the ladders seem to wobble
and bulge?

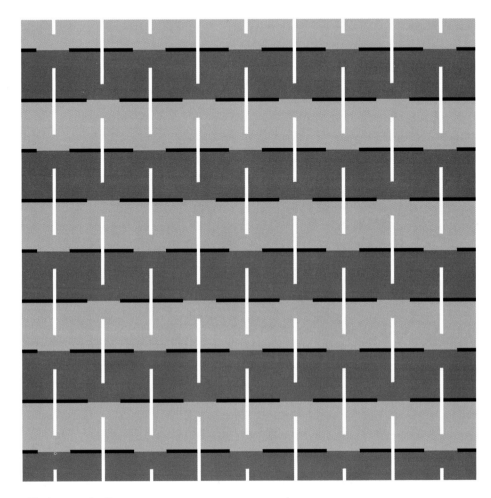

Christmas balls

Do you see illusory light bicolor discs in this pattern?

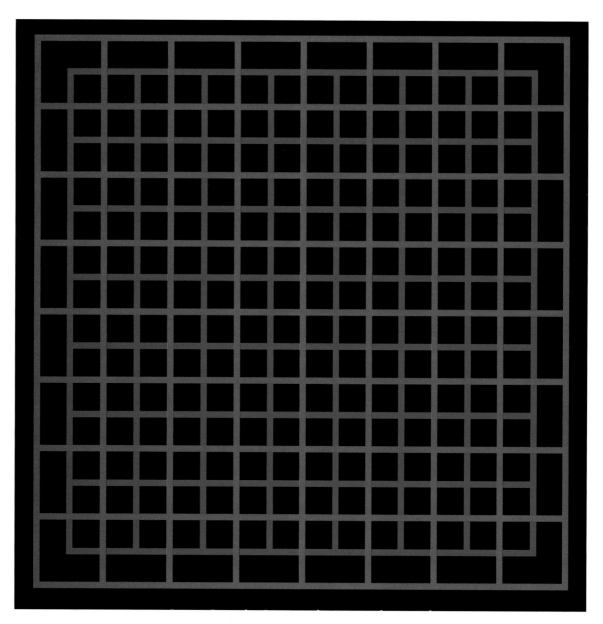

3D grids

Do you see tridimensional grids? Is the red grid slightly distorted?

Glowing and scintillating

Shift your gaze around the picture. You may see ghost discs glowing at the intersection points of the bars while clear bright spots pop up in their middles.

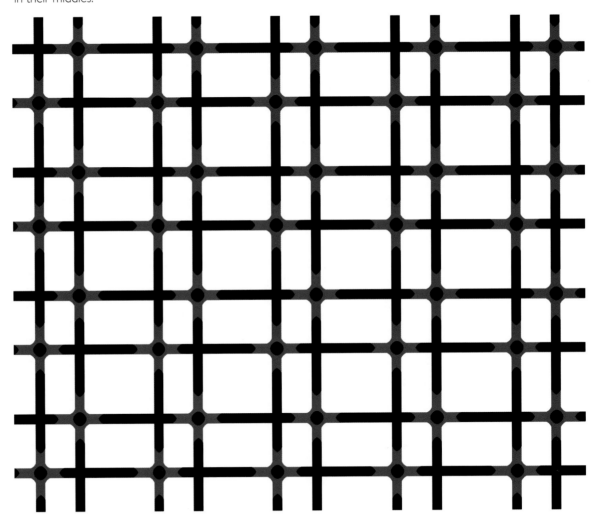

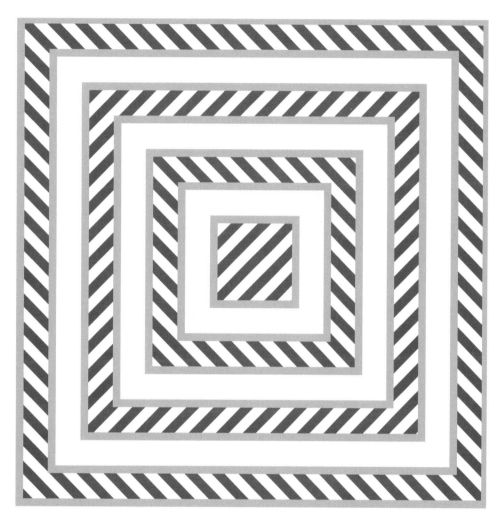

Tilted frames
Are the squares skewed?

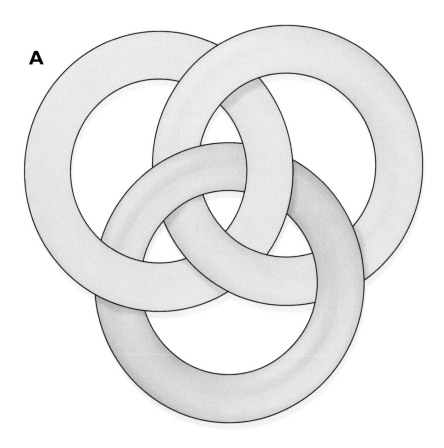

A

Borromean rings
Can three flat circles be interlinked
as shown in A? Can you do the
same with three paper clips?

B

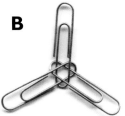

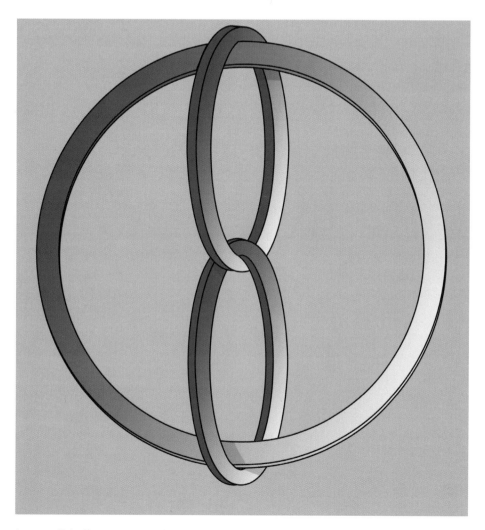

Impossible Borromean rings
An impossible 3D figure.

Gallery VI Notes

Page 144
Shape distortion can occur when contrasting objects are nearby. Yes, it's a perfect circle, though the points of the stars induce the circle to appear slightly flat. Actually, each set of four stars delimitates a square. Do you perceive them?

Page 145
As our tendency is to see vertical objects as more slender than horizontal objects, the parallelogram shape which forms the horizontal axis of the cross appears larger than the parallelogram shape forming the vertical axis. So we perceive segment CD slightly larger than segment AB, despite the fact they are the same length.

Page 146
The special asymmetric shape of the flakes is responsible for these illusions, but the lines are perfectly parallel. Here is an additional effect: if you shift your gaze around the flakes for a while, you may see a gray spot appear inside each flock.

Page 148
Line A.

Page 149
The shapes are perfect squares. Strangely enough, when perfect squares are assembled in regular sets, they tend to lose their regularity. The illusion works better when it is seen from a certain distance.

Page 150
Vision depends on the tiny imperceptible eye movements which keep the visual stimulus constant. In the picture, the gradual color difference from gray to blue is a poor stimulus for sustaining visual perception. However, if your eyes freely move over the stimulus, the perception of it will be sustained. When you fixate on the dark blue dot (the nose of the cat) and try holding your gaze as steady as possible, then the haze should fade away and the color of the background will predominate. The re-apparition of the cat will be triggered by a decisive eye movement.

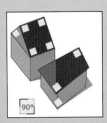

Page 151
8! Generally people manage to locate up to 6 right angles easily. A tough one to find is that on the upper side of the house in the background. Two or three 90-degree angles don't look very convincing, but this is entirely due to a trick of the apparent perspective.

Page 152
Both are the same size. This is a neat variant of the Ponzo illusion.

Page 153
The rungs of every second ladder are out of phase, causing this wobbling or bulging effect. This illusion is similar to the Café wall illusion.

Page 154
Light circular discs with phantom contours can be perceived over the empty spaces between the black and white lines. Scientists have proved that this kind of brightness illusion is not created in the retina, but as a consequence of interaction between both optic nerves in the higher regions of the brain cortex.
Both the phantom edge phenomenon shown in the picture (also called the Ehrenstein illusion) and the Kanisza figure illusion are triggered by the T-effect; there are groups of neural cells which react to line ends and without further input, create the intersections to the horizontal bar of the letter T as a precautionary measure. Each intersection could indicate the concealment of a figure in the foreground, so recognition of a potential danger must be rapid. If various T elements indicate a distinct figure (eg. circle, square), the ghost contour is drawn in the head and the core of the figure is filled in with either the lightened or darkened background.

Page 155
No; obviously the grids are all located on the same plane. Brightness and color influence distance perception; bright, warm colors tend to be seen as closer than cold colors, creating a tridimensional effect.

Page 156
This illusion combines the Lingelbach grid effect with the Van Tuijl neon color illusion.

Page 157
No; they are perfectly aligned and parallel. Take a ruler and see for yourself! This is a kind of Zöllner illusion.

Page 158
If you try making the Borromean rings out of wire, you will find that you cannot make the figure with real flat circles. There must always be kinks. The theorem stating Borromean rings to be

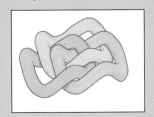

impossible with flat circles is proved in the article "Borromean circles are impossible" *American Mathematics Monthly*, 98 (1991), by B. Lindström and H.O. Zetterström.

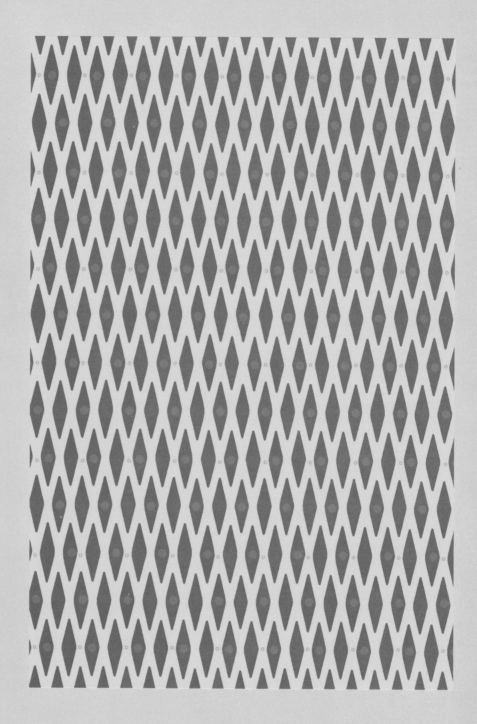

Vanishing dots

Can you count all the dots present in this hypnotic pattern? It is very difficult to perceive the small dots at the crossings of the grid because they tend to disappear spontaneously when you scan the image; likewise for the light dots in the rhombi.

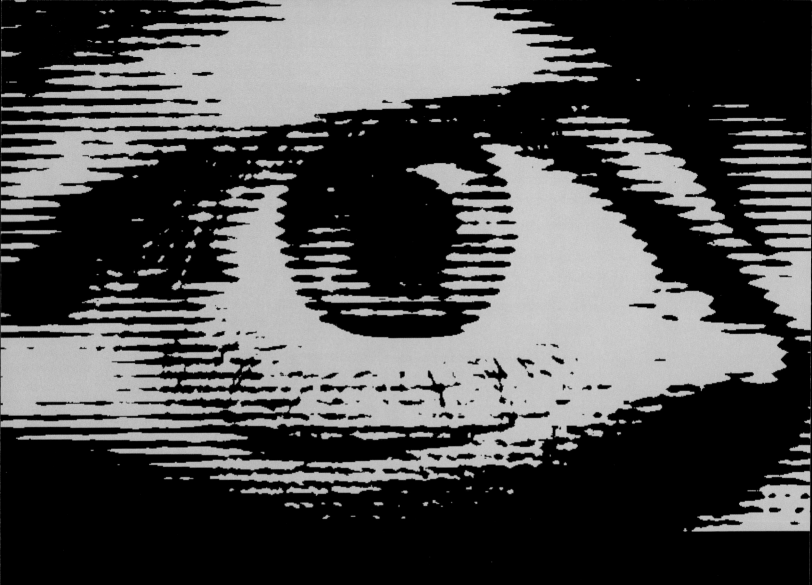

Gallery VII

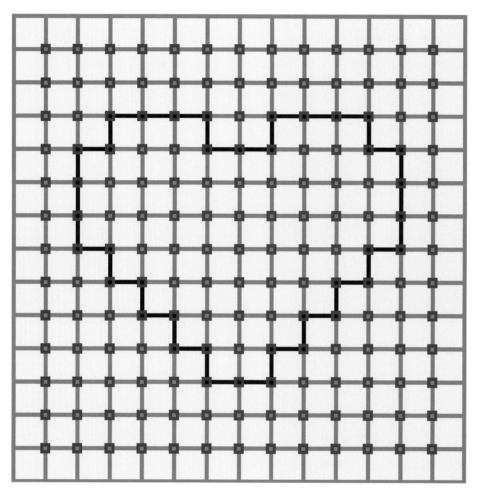

Neon Heart

Can you see an orange neon heart with a bright halo around it? View the picture from a good distance.
The color in the background is perfectly uniform. The apparent orange color is created by the interaction of the black lines with the yellow background, and the apparent white halo by the interaction of the blue lines with the small dark squares.

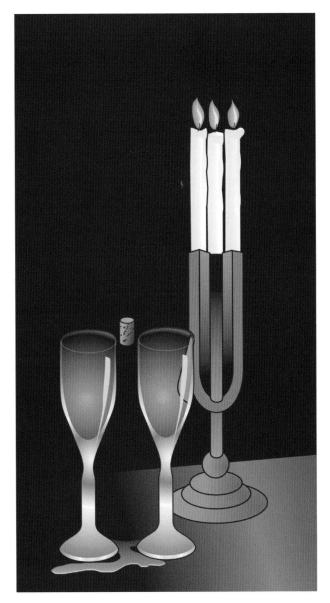

Just two anomalies
There was a party, but where is the bottle? Do
you see another oddity?

Cloud Test

With just one stroke, transform these clouds into a forest.

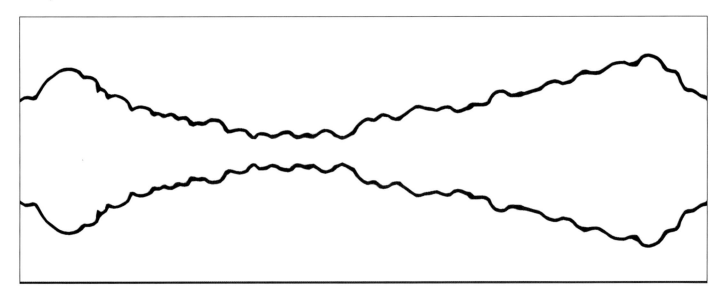

Greek temple

Cut the puzzle (remember to copy it first!)
into two pieces in order to make a column of
the temple vanish when the pieces are
perfectly rearranged. Impossible?

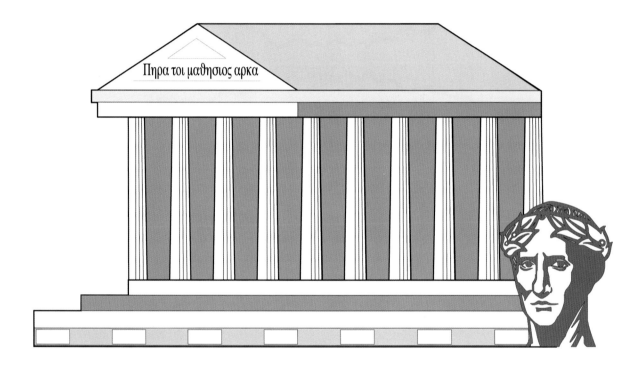

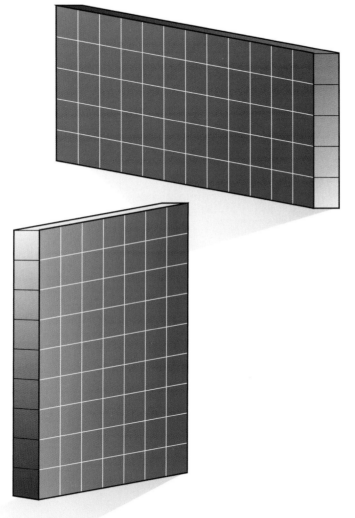

Low walls
Are the blue surfaces of the low walls different? Can you calculate their area?

Visual fitting test

Which shape (A, B, or C) fits exactly into
the pentagonal hole?

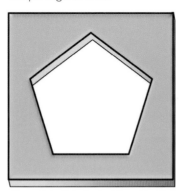

A

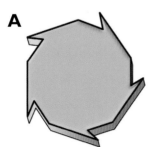

B

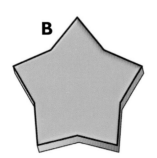

C

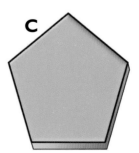

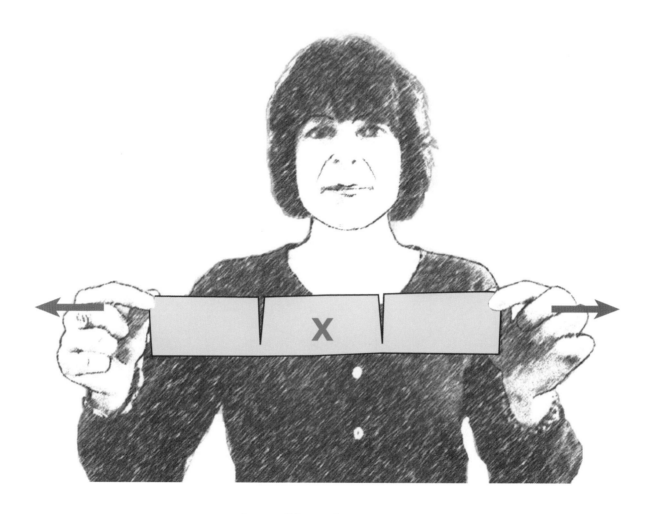

Impossible tearings

Take a strip of paper and make two
incisions in it as shown in the
picture. Hold the strip by its ends and pull
in order to break the strip.
What is the probability that the central
piece marked with an X falls
out: 1/3, 2/3, or 3/3?

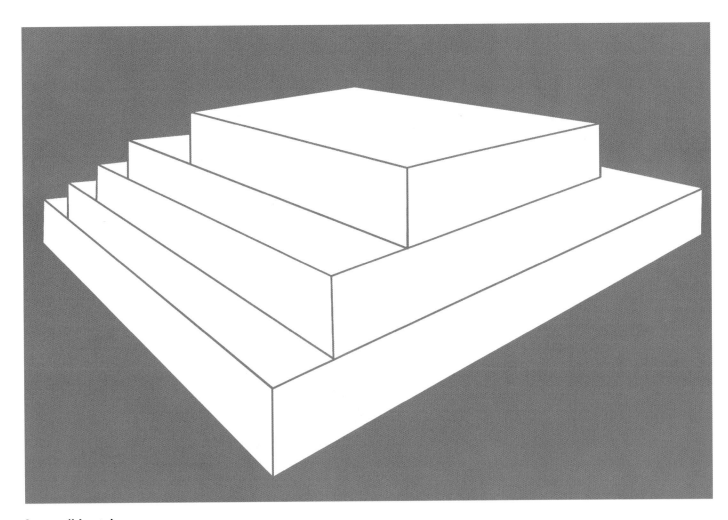

Impossible stairs

Arrows

Is the red arrow longer or shorter than the blue one?

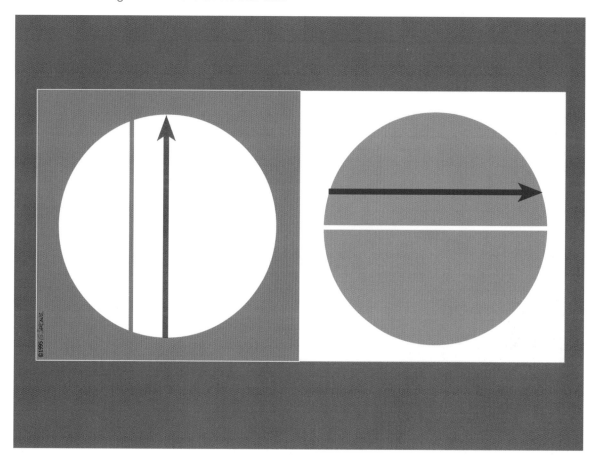

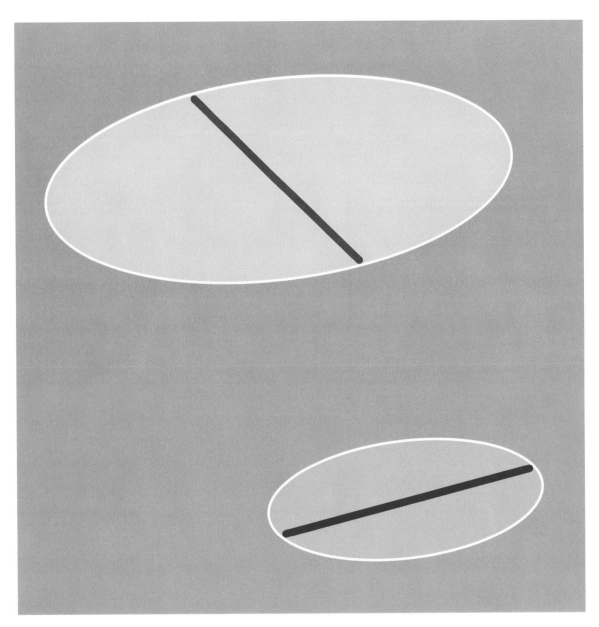

Deceptive ellipses
Which line seems longer, the red one or the
blue one?

Line A = Line B?

Are lines A and B really the same length?

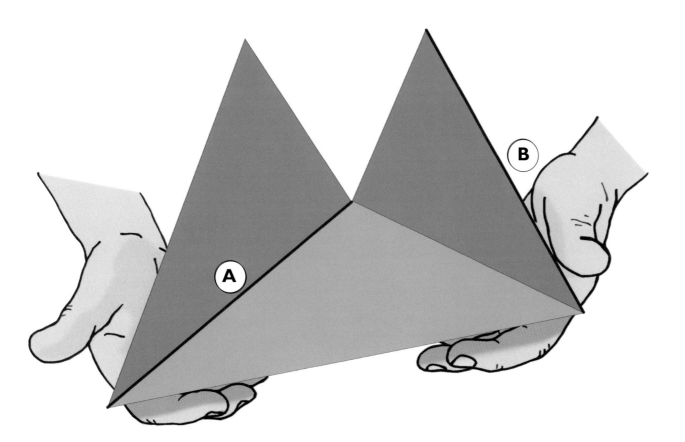

Curved lines

Which arc segment has the greatest radius of curvature, A or B?

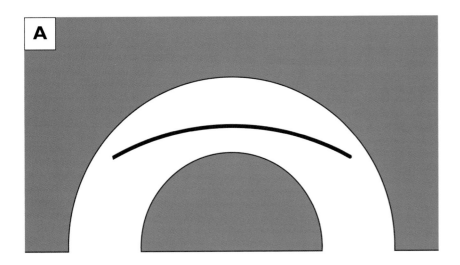

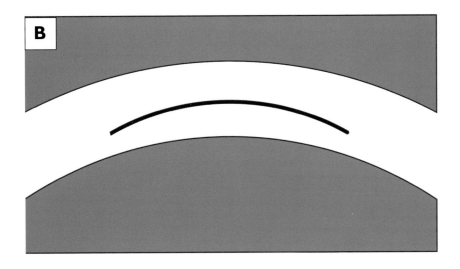

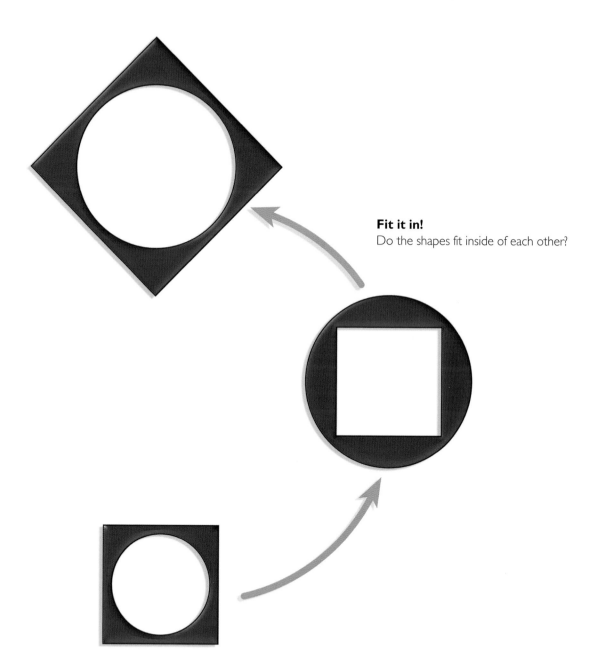

Fit it in!
Do the shapes fit inside of each other?

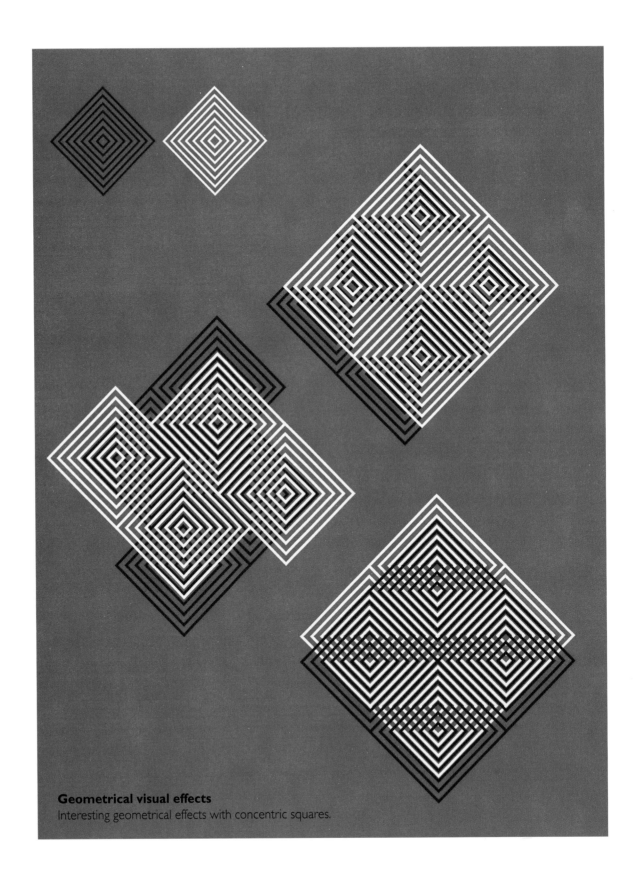

Geometrical visual effects
Interesting geometrical effects with concentric squares.

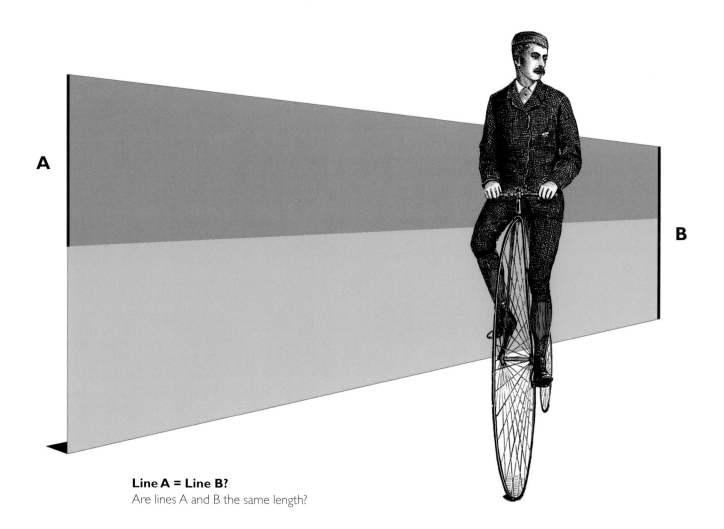

A

B

Line A = Line B?
Are lines A and B the same length?

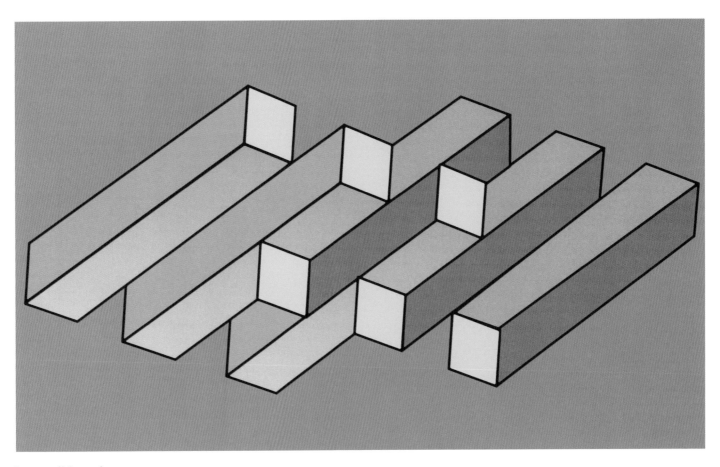

Impossible rods

Which group of rods is on top in the picture and which one is underneath?

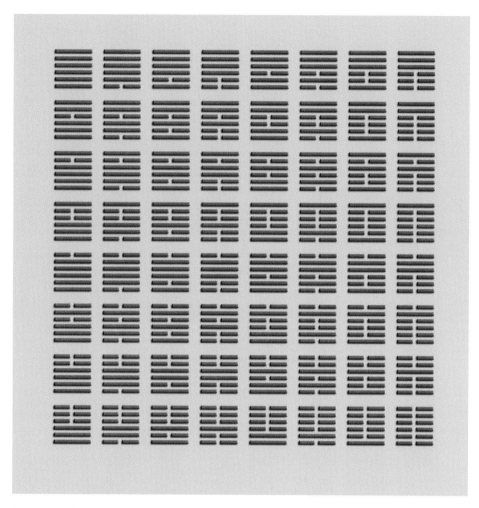

Vibrating I-Ching

Illustrated in the picture are the 64 I-Ching symbols. These antique signs are part of Chinese philosophy. But they can also produce optical illusions. Do you see gray spots between the I-Ching symbols? Do you perceive some vertical flows? These effects are induced by lateral inhibition of our visual system.

Side A = Side B?
Which side seems shorter, side A or side B?

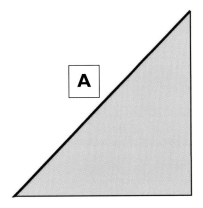

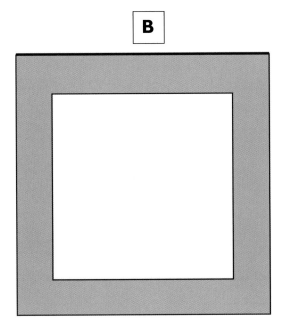

Line A = Line B?
Line B seems longer... but are you sure?

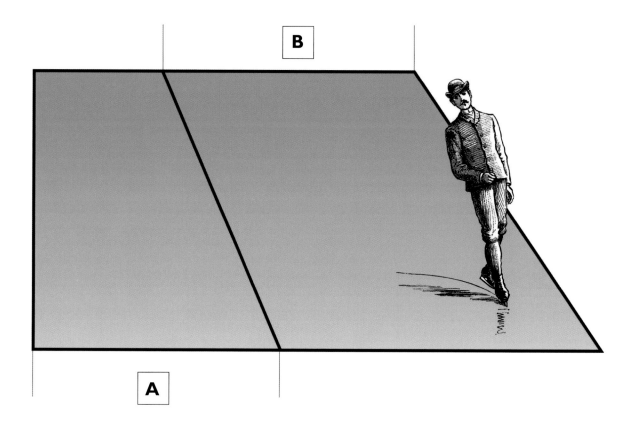

The upside-down sentence is TRUE *si ǝɔuǝʇuǝs uмop - ǝpısdn ǝɥꓕ*

Visual logic paradox

This is either an ambigram (turn the page upside-down),
or a self-referential paradox. Now ponder whether the sentence is
true or false.

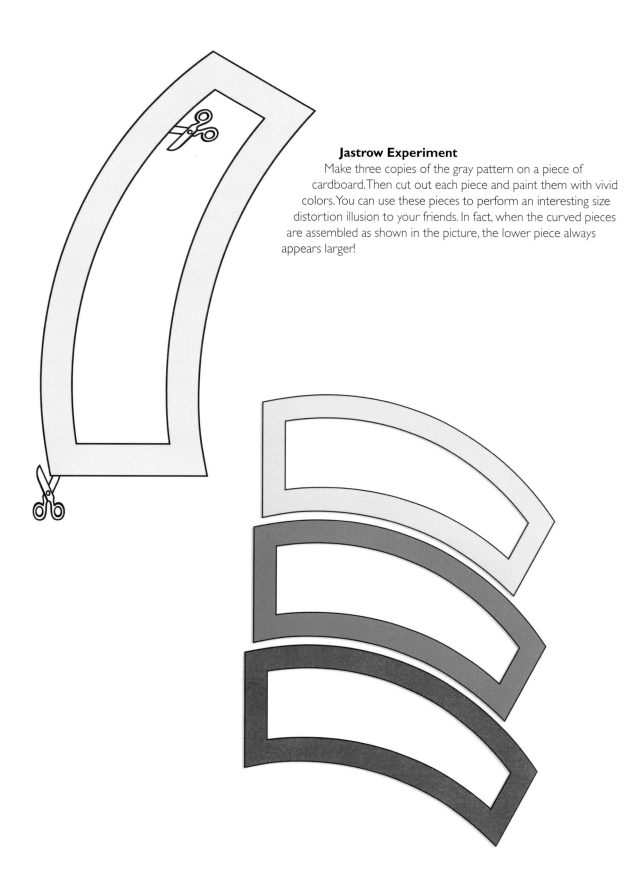

Jastrow Experiment

Make three copies of the gray pattern on a piece of cardboard. Then cut out each piece and paint them with vivid colors. You can use these pieces to perform an interesting size distortion illusion to your friends. In fact, when the curved pieces are assembled as shown in the picture, the lower piece always appears larger!

Gallery VII Notes

Page 164

The bottle is concealed between the two glasses. The other oddity is that it is impossible to say if the candelabra has two or three sticks.

Page 165

Here is a forest reflected in a mountain lake.

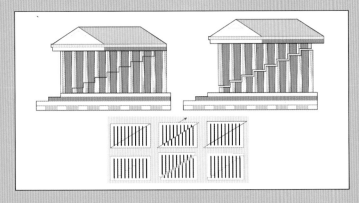

Page 166

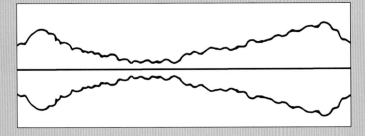

Page 167

Visually, the first wall seems to have an area of (12 × 5 =) 60 square units; and the second one, an area of (7 × 9 =) 63 square units. But actually, the blue surfaces are identical in shape and size, even though they look different! This illusion is related to the "crossing parallelogram" illusion. To find the real area of the blue surfaces, called parallelograms, you have to multiply their **base** by their **height**.

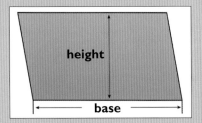

Page 168

Shape A!

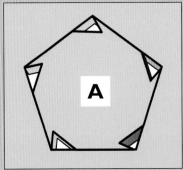

Page 169

The probability that the central piece marked with a X falls out is 0/3! This is the illustration of an improper use of probabilities for a physical event. We are simply deceived by our common sense.

Page 171

Red arrow = blue arrow!

Page 172

The blue line is longer than the red one. Measure them!

Page 173

Yes, they are.

Page 174

In fact, the arc segments are identical. The context in which the arc is placed determines its appearance.

Page 175

No, none can be fitted in to another!

Page 177

Yes, they are the same length, despite the fact they look different. This is a variant of the Ponzo illusion.

Page 178

It is impossible to determine which group of rods is on top. These are just impossible figures.

Page 180

The hypotenuse A of the triangle seems shorter than the side B of the square. However, they are the same length.

Page 181

Line A = Line B.

Page 182

This contradictory sentence is not resolvable in conventional logic systems. But not all self-referential sentences are paradoxical: consider 'this sentence is true.'

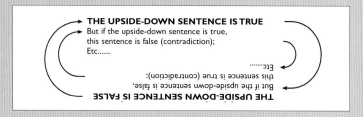

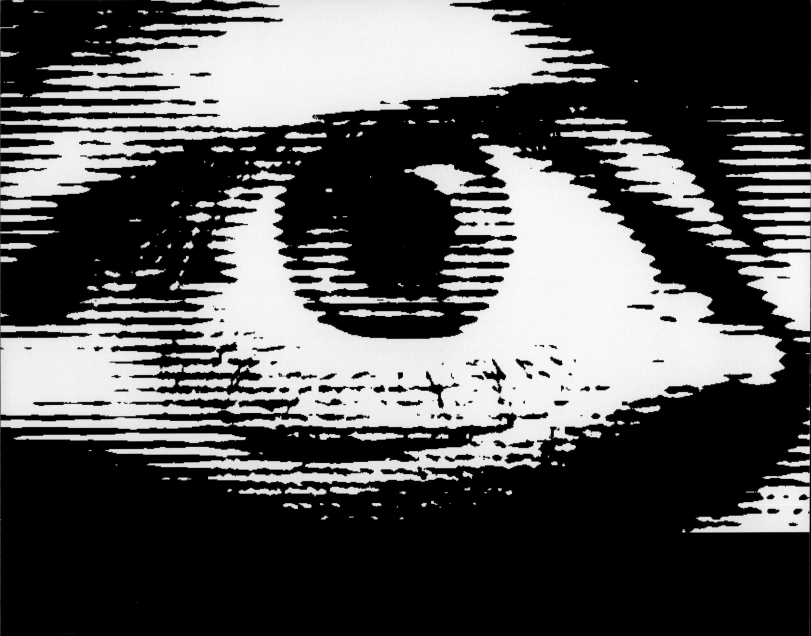

Gallery VIII

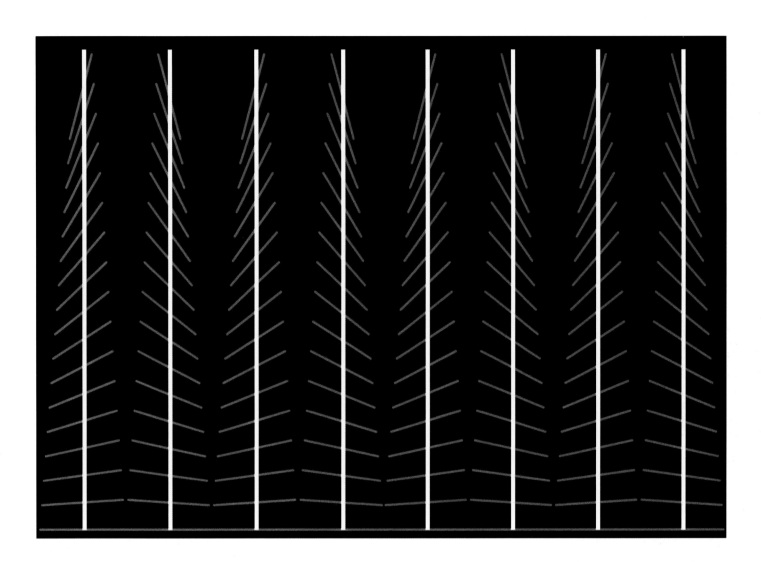

Distorted lines
Do the lines tend to bend in at the top? No; it's just an illusion!

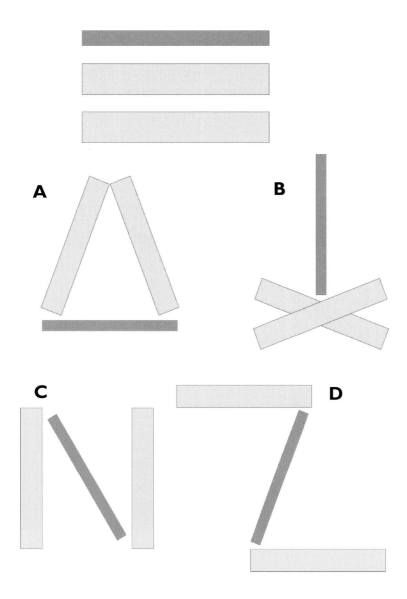

Paper strips

Make two sets of three paper strips as shown in the picture and make figures A and B. Strangely, in configuration A, the thinner paper strip looks shorter than the thicker paper strips; in B, the effect is reversed! Finally make figures C and D; curiously, the paper strip in the middle looks longer in configuration D. Try this experiment with your friends!

Impossible stairs 2

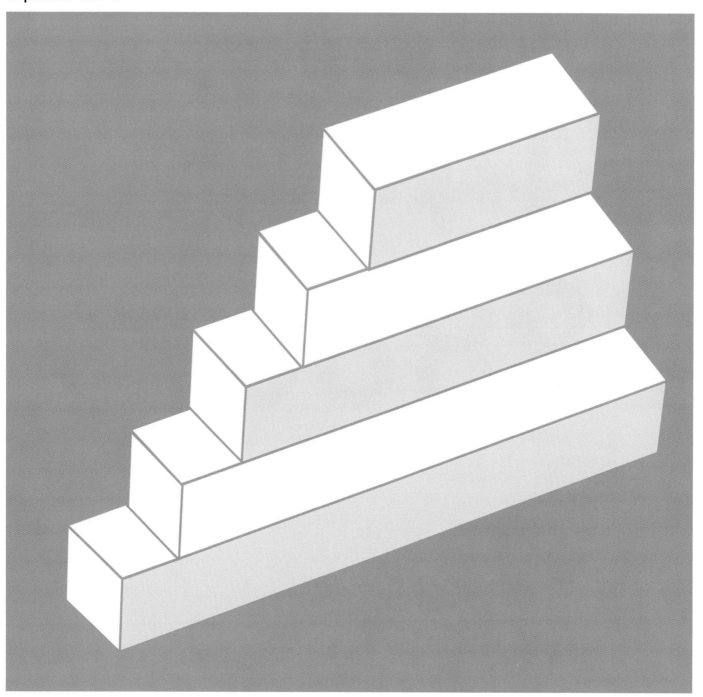

444444

888888

Fours and eights

Consider the two rows of numbers. Are all the 4s the same thickness?
What about the eights?

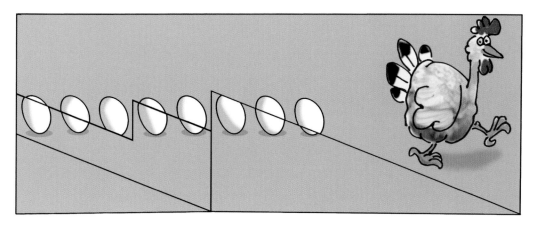

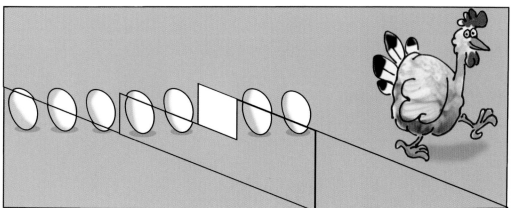

Befuddling Chicken and Eggs Puzzle

Which came first, the chicken or the egg? Well, the problem here is: who "stole" the egg from Chiquita, our favorite chicken? As you can see in the four-piece puzzle in A, there are eight eggs…

Now if we move some of the puzzle pieces around (B), an egg disappears along with a portion of the puzzle. But the missing portion doesn't have an egg on it!

How does this work?

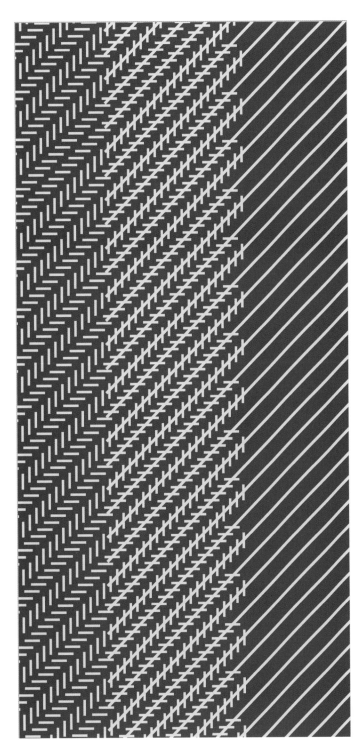

Zöllner revisited

The conjunction of parallel lines and sets of oblique strokes creates an interesting distortion illusion.

Tracing star

First, photocopy the star. Then, take a pencil and trace a line within its borders while you are looking in the mirror at your drawing. You can hide the drawing with a book as shown in the picture. Find it easy?

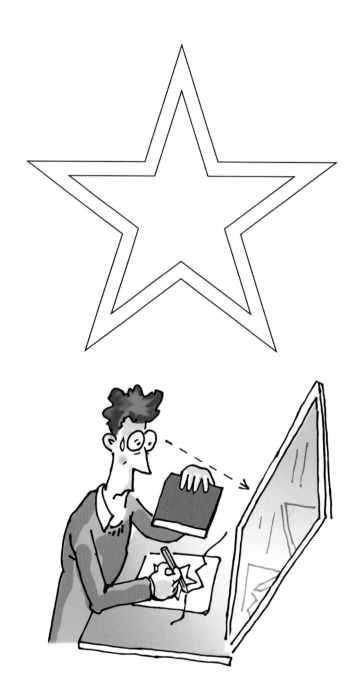

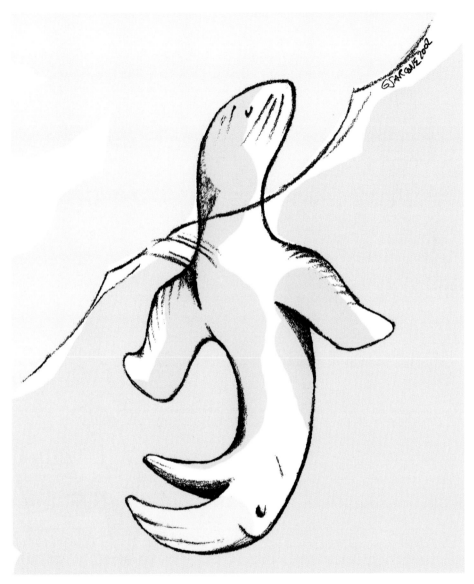

Seal or...?
Can you see how to transform a marine mammal into a flying animal?

Solitude
Is the old lady really alone? How many people are with her?

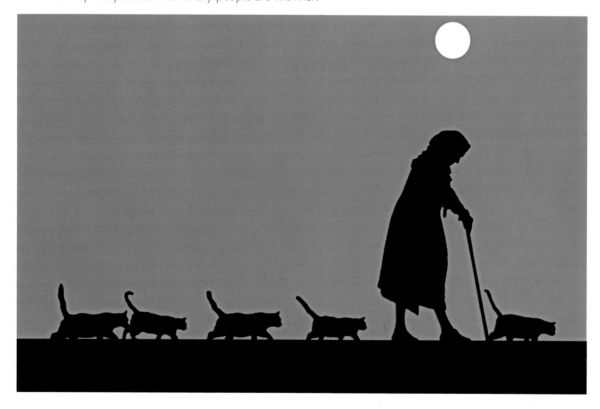

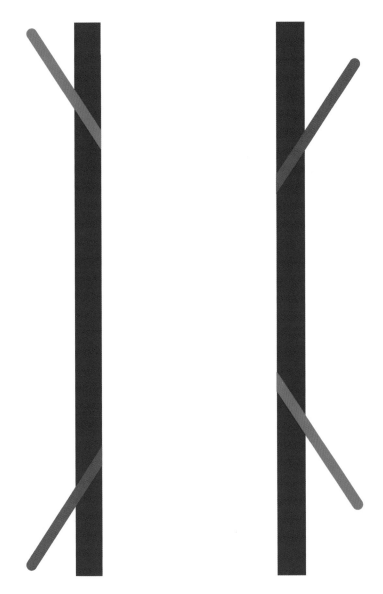

Aligned?

Which line segments aren't aligned correctly to form a straight line, the magenta or the green ones?

Lines

Is the blue line longer than any of the red lines?

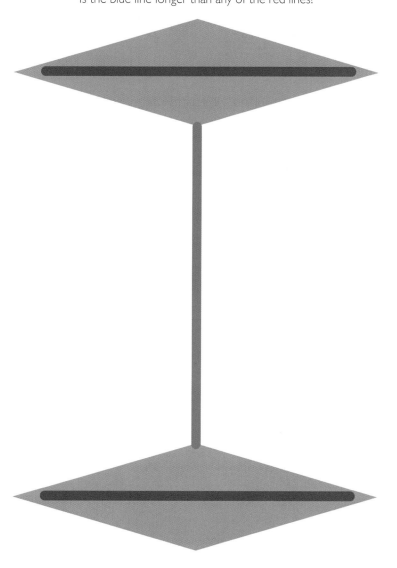

A

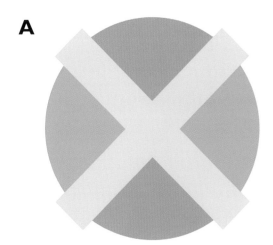

Sliced Colors
Consider both colored figures in A and B. In which case (A or B) are the vertical green slices the same shade as the horizontal slices?

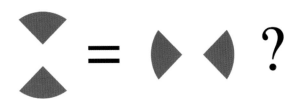

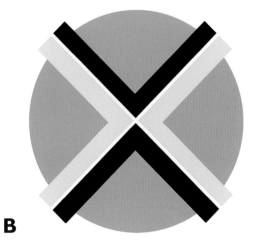

B

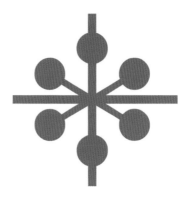

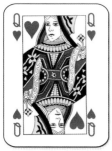

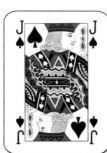

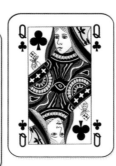

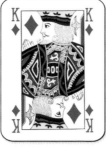

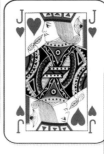

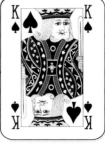

Visual Memory test

Concentrate on both red and green symbols for ten seconds. Now select one of the playing cards – any of them – and firmly concentrate on it. Memorize your card, then turn the page over!

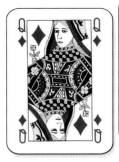 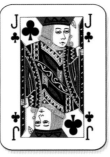 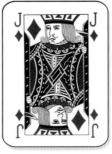 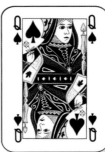 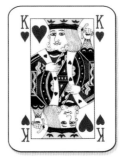

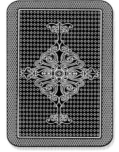

Magic cards
Believe it or not,
the card you
selected has been
removed from the
assortment and
turned over. Right?

A

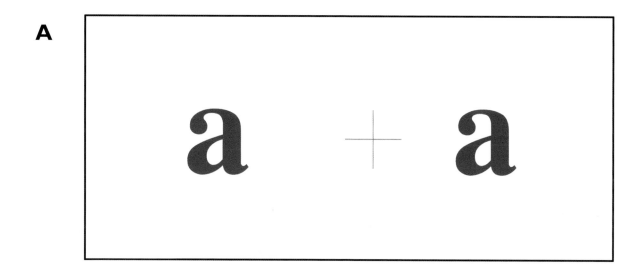

B

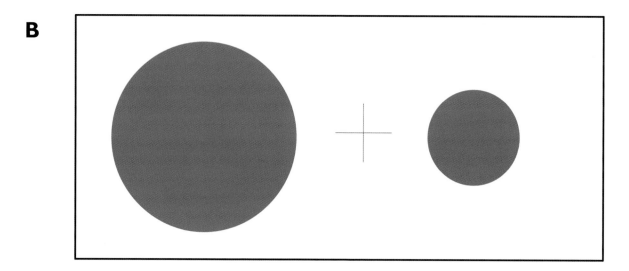

Bold the A

To enlarge one of the 'a' letters shown in diagram A, stare at the dots
in diagram B for about 20-30 seconds, then look at the letters
'a.' You should see a letter becoming larger and bolder!
(The experiment works better under bright light.)

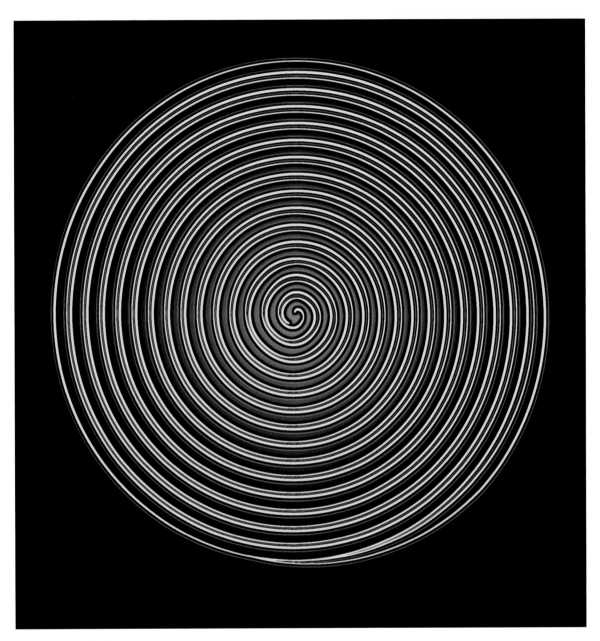

Concentric circles

Concentrate on the upper part of the disc; can you determine if it contains concentric circles or just a spiral? Is the disc perfectly circular?

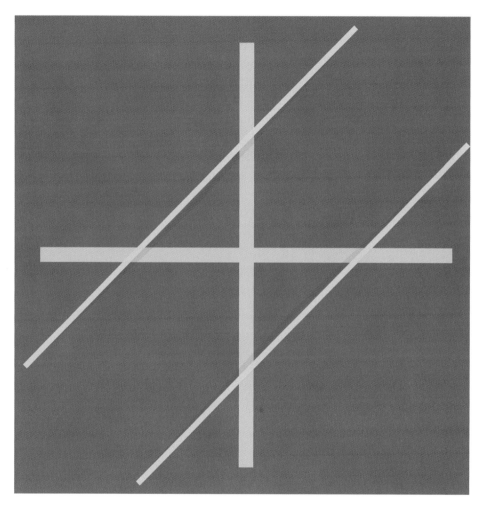

Parallel or not? 1
Are the yellow lines bulging outwards?

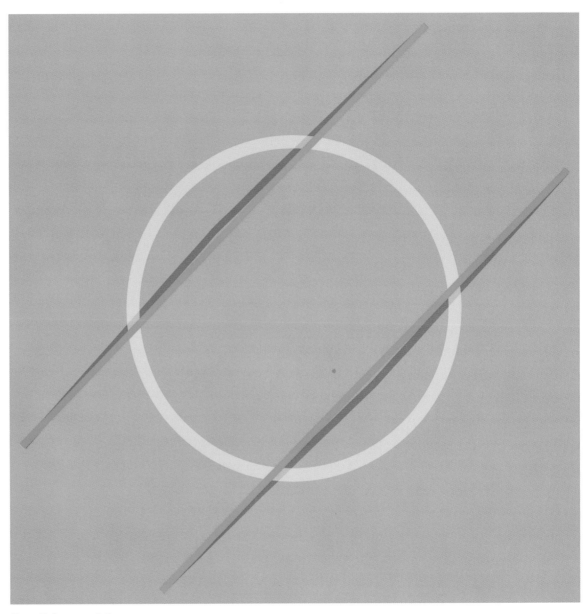

Parallel or not? 2
Are the green lines straight and parallel to each other?

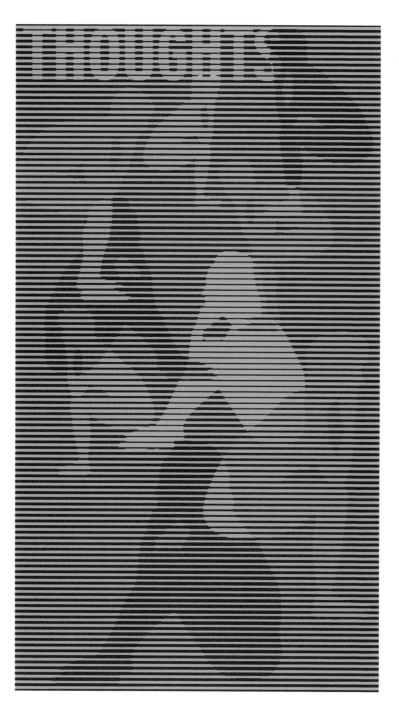

Floating thoughts
Do you see the shapes of floating, thinking men and women? It's just your imagination...

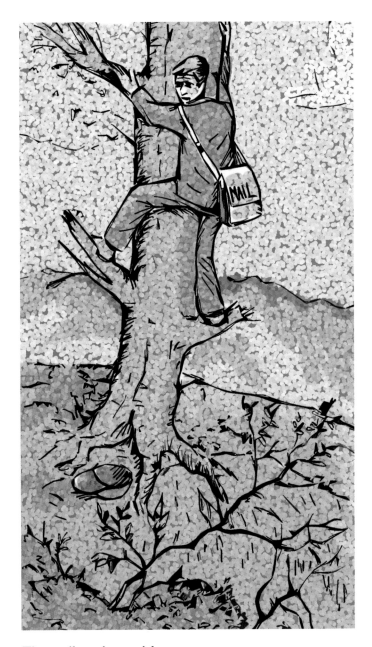

The mailman's anguish
What does every mailman fear?

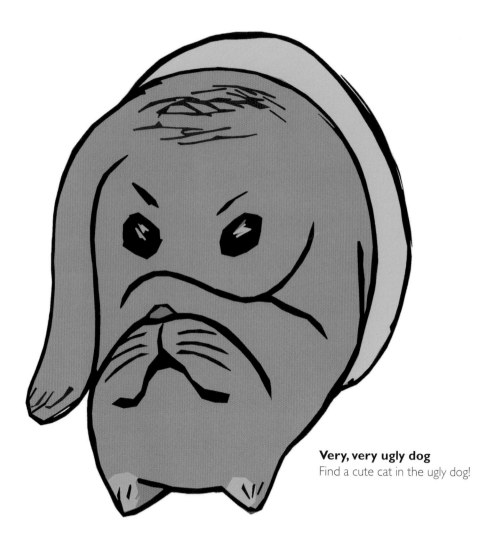

Very, very ugly dog
Find a cute cat in the ugly dog!

Gallery VIII Notes

Page 190
The three 4s on the right are slightly larger, while the 8s are all the same thickness. The second set of 8s on the right was just turned upside-down.

Page 191
Reassembling puzzles which include triangular pieces may lead to paradoxical conclusions! In this particular case, we have two paradoxes in one when both triangular pieces of the puzzle are inverted:

1. a substantial portion of the puzzle seems to be missing;
2. an egg has vanished.

Of course, apparent gain or loss of area is offset by a complementary loss or gain elsewhere in the puzzle. The loss of the small surface is due to the fact that the bases of the triangles aren't perfectly aligned to form a continuous straight line at the bottom of the puzzle. In figure A, the point where the triangles meet is slightly retracted, whereas in B it is protruding. The area of the 'missing' surface in B is simply redistributed within this prominent line. And what about the missing egg?
By switching the triangular pieces of the puzzle the egg doesn't disappear at all – a fraction of the image is redistributed among the seven eggs that remain. Can you see that the seven remaining eggs in B are slightly longer than the eight eggs shown in A?
This puzzle, involving the vanishing of a surface, as well as the vanishing of a graphic element, is an original novelty invented by the mathemagician Gianni A. Sarcone. You may have heard of him somewhere before!

Page 193
Tracing a drawing with the help of a mirror can be very confusing for our procedural memory. The procedural memory is our motion memory. When performing something with procedural memory, one is not consciously aware of exactly how one is performing each individual movement or how to combine the movements. Becoming aware of these things can disrupt a well-learned skill. Now, when you try to draw something by looking in a mirror, you have to inhibit and reverse all that is associated with vision and motion control (and as you have experienced yourself, the first time it is very, very difficult!).

Page 194
Just turn the image upside-down and you will discover a toucan.

Page 195
You can see the presence of five faces in the tails of the cats.

Page 196
The green segments aren't properly aligned to form a straight, continuous line.

Page 197
The lines are all the same length. This is a Müller-Lyer illusion variant.

Page 198
In A, the vertical slices are different from the horizontal slices.

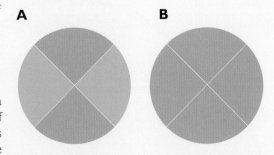

Pages 199–200
This trick is simply based on visual memory. Hint: people concentrate on the selected card but not on the surrounding playing cards…

Page 201
This is an original after-effect experiment.

Page 202
The disc contains just a spiral and isn't circular at all.

Page 203
No; they are perfectly straight and parallel to each other. This distortion illusion is induced by the cross in the background.

Page 204
Even though they seem to bulge inwards, they are perfectly straight and parallel to each other. This distortion illusion is induced by the circle in the background.

Page 205
There are no really determined shapes in the drawing; just lines and illusory figures!

Page 206
A dog! Find it in the bush at the bottom of the illustration.

Page 207
To find it, just rotate the image counterclockwise by a quarter-turn.

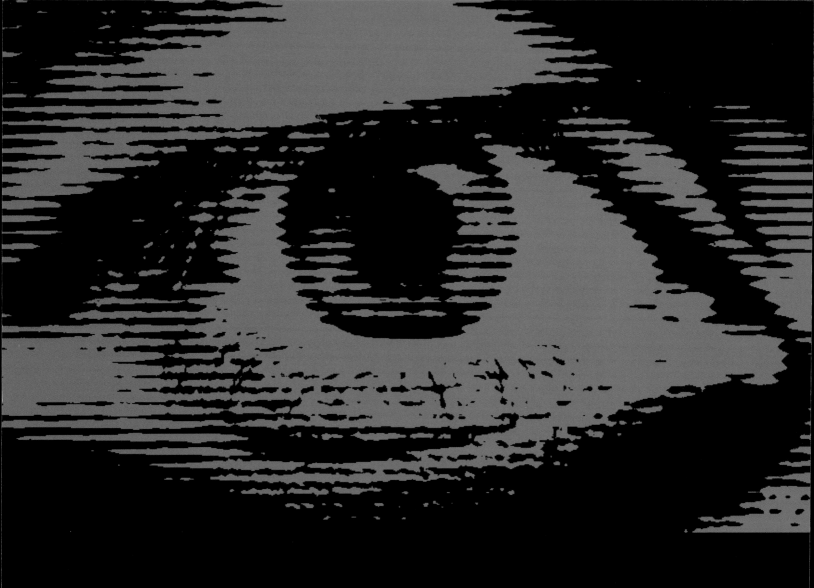

Gallery IX

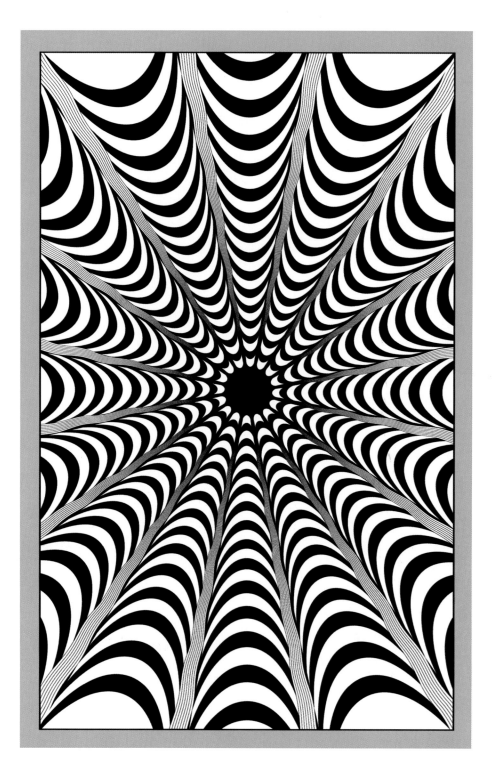

Good vibrations
Do you see some converging vibrating flows? No, you aren't seeing things; it's just a natural lateral inhibition effect...

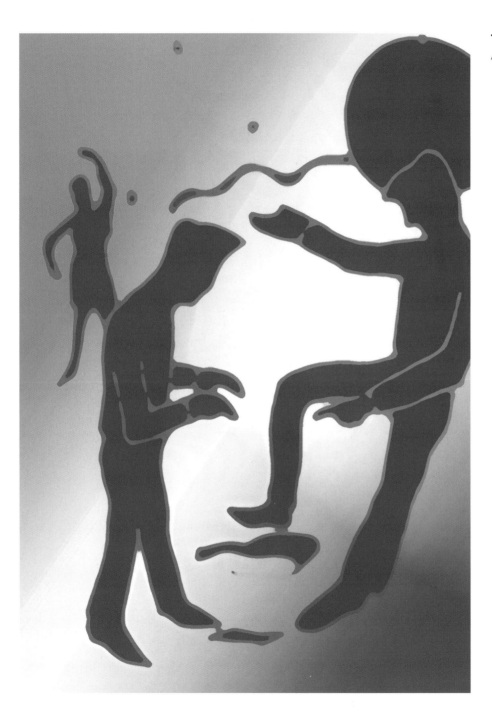

The lonely dancers
Are they really lonely?

Impossible eight-point star?

Cut slits in two single, square paper sheets so that, when the sheets are interlaced, they form the eight-pointed star figure.

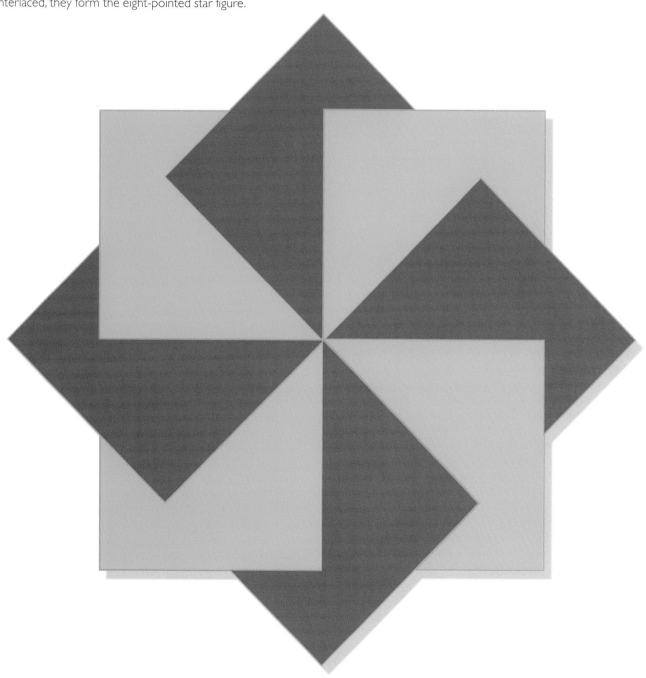

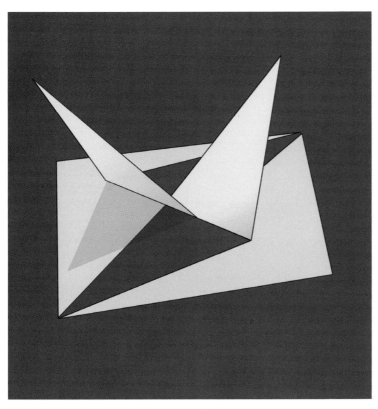

Impossible foldings 1

Are you able to reproduce this tridimensional figure just by cutting and folding a single piece of strong paper?

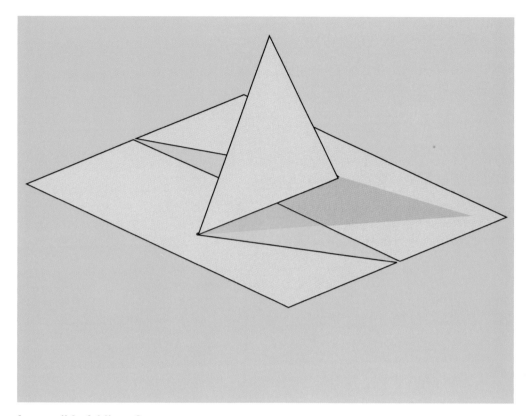

Impossible foldings 2

Can you reproduce this pyramid-like figure just by cutting and folding
a single piece of strong paper? (You cannot cut the paper into two or
more different pieces.)

Impossible Stairs 3

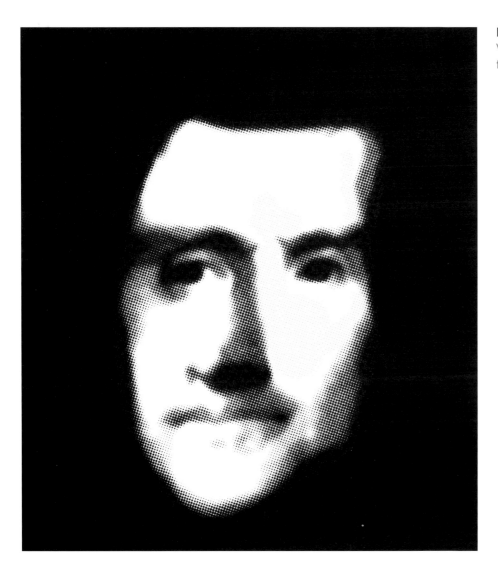

Living eyes
Wherever you are, this face seems to follow you with its eyes.

Gray gradations

Color gradations can affect the alignment of regular objects. In the picture, the squares are perfectly aligned and parallel!

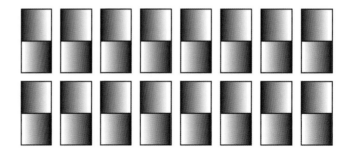

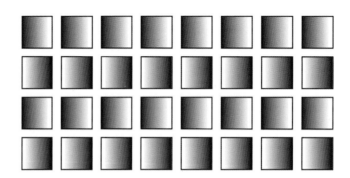

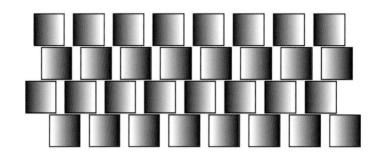

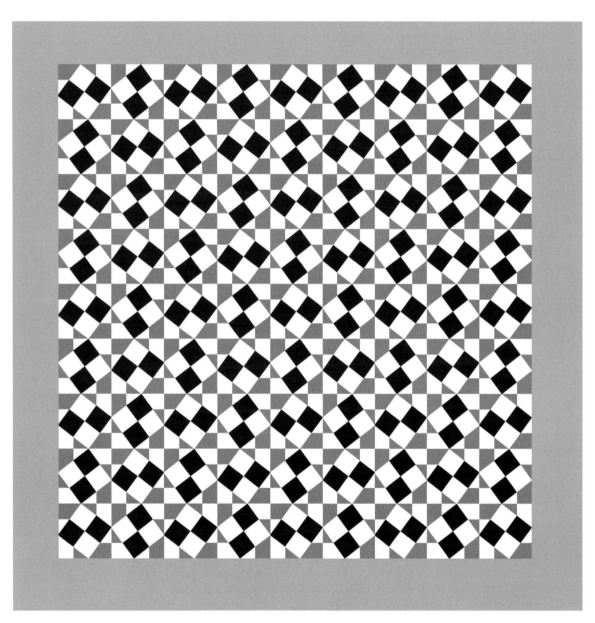

Round corners?

The checkered, small squares seem to have wobbly, round corners. Squares tend to lose their evenness when assembled in regular sets (see also "Squeezed squares").

Boing visual patterns

An interesting visual effect of coaxial circles and ellipses is created by placing a negative arrangement of concentric black and white circles with an 'invert blending mode' on an alignment of black and white stripes. Changing the thickness of the stripes in the background alters the image dramatically, as illustrated in the three examples.

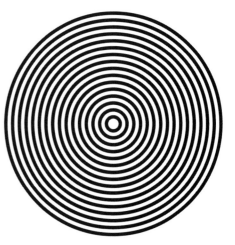

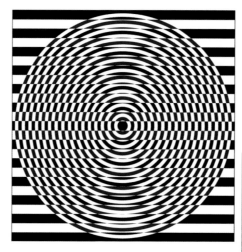

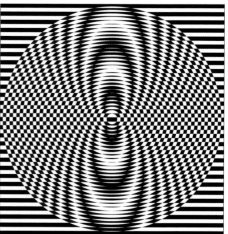

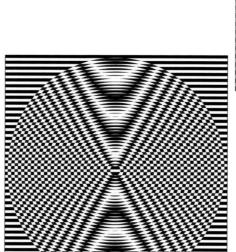

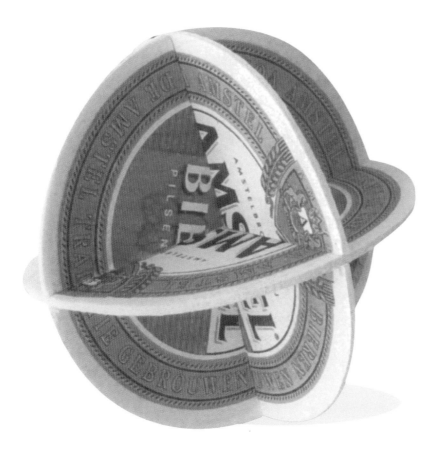

Make a magic cardboard ball
Take three circular mats or pieces of stiff cardboard and try to assemble them as shown in the picture. The figure is made by cutting and interlocking three single pieces together without glue or adhesive of any kind. Is this figure possible?

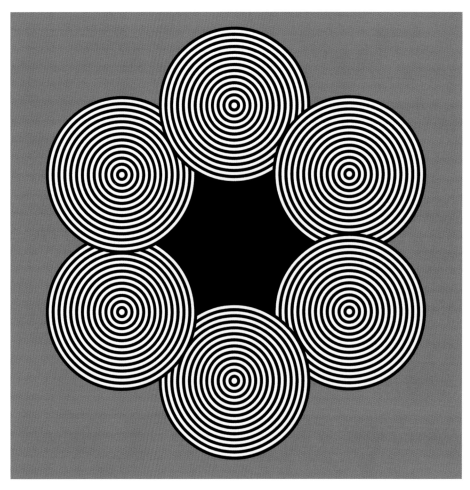

Moving concentric pattern
Concentric regular arrangements cause visual perturbations.
The picture seems to vibrate.

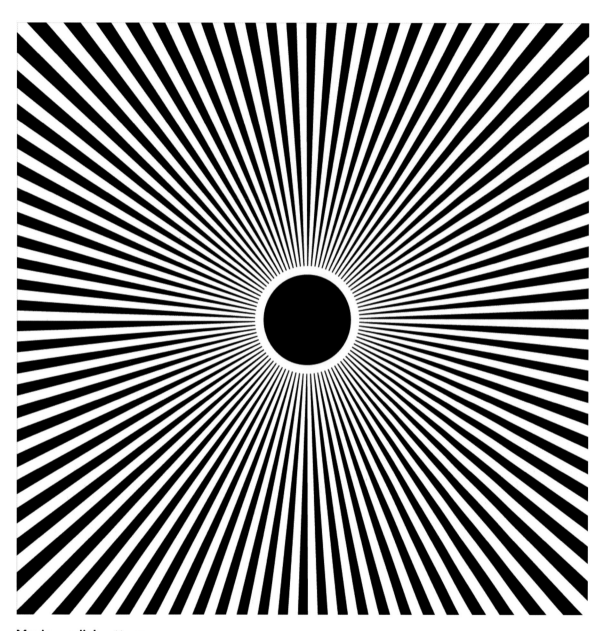

Moving radial pattern

Radial patterns can induce visual perturbations. The image seems to shimmer when the page is moved slightly. If you move your eyes around the spokes, you may even see color appear.

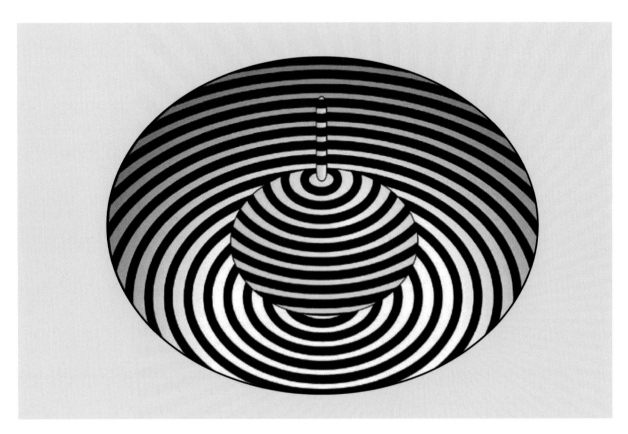

Magic top
Move the picture from side to side to make the top spin.

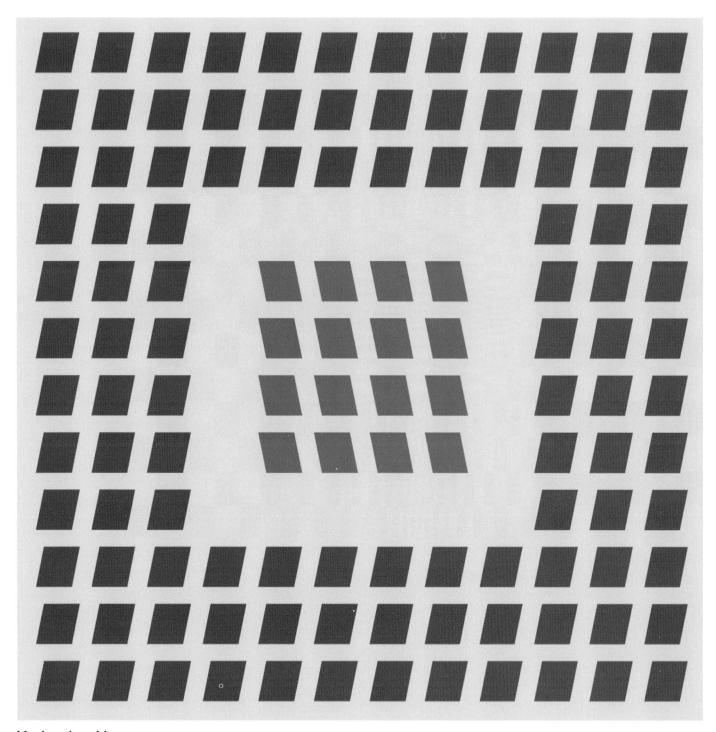

Moving rhombi

If you shake the image slightly, the inset of blue rhombi starts moving independently of the background and the surrounding orange rhombi.

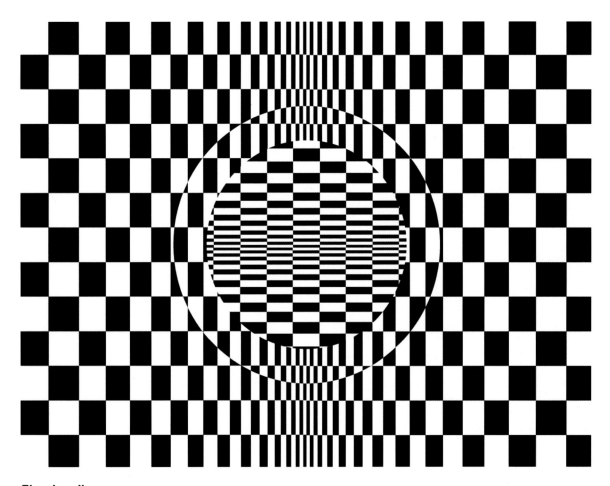

Floating disc

Observe the image and concentrate on the central disc, while shaking the image slightly. The circular shape appears to separate from the rest of the picture and levitate above the checkered background.

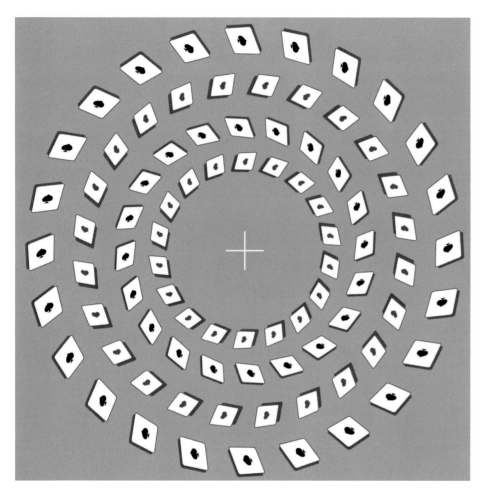

Rotating circles

The circular sets of playing cards seem to counter-rotate when you move your head backwards and forwards, keeping your focus on the cross in the center of the image. Do you notice something odd?

Horizontal fluids

Do the curved lines seem to vibrate and blink forwards and backwards?

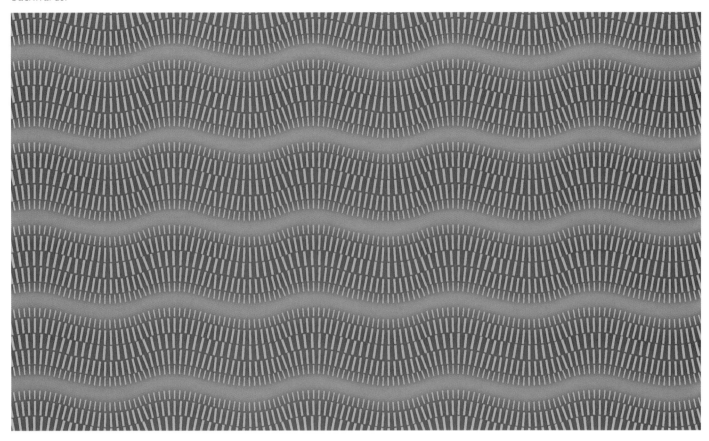

Fill the van

Is it possible to fit all these boxes into the van? If not, which pieces cannot be included?

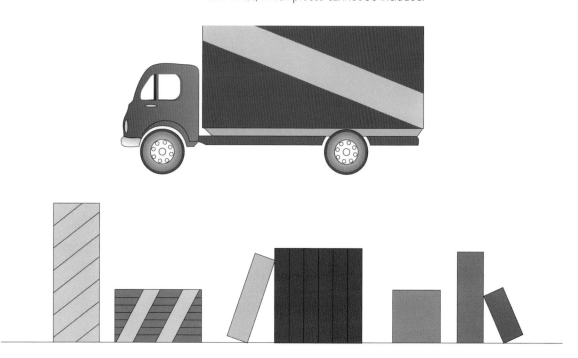

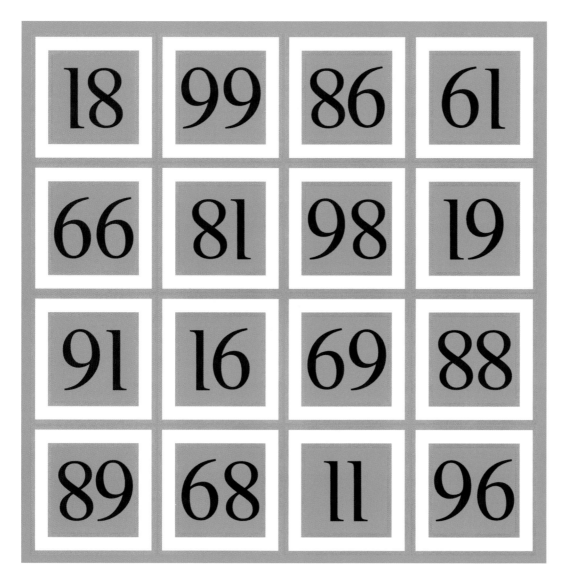

Magic magic square

Magic squares are squares filled in by aligned numbers with the characteristic that the sum of the numbers of each row, column, and diagonal is the same. The square featured in this page is a magic magic square. Why?

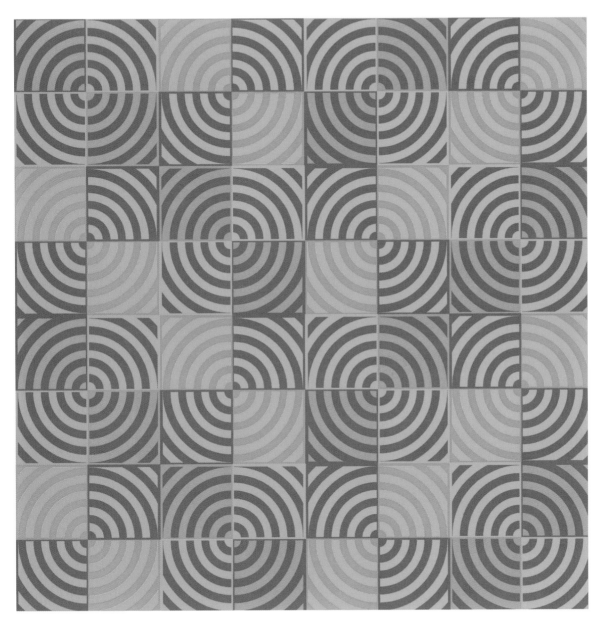

Color patchwork

Move two meters (six feet) away from this picture and you will see two apparent colors: blue and yellow. But if you observe them closely, you will notice that they are actually orange and green!

Gallery IX Notes

Page 212

A womans face can be perceived at the center of the illustration. This is an ambiguous figure-ground illusion.

Page 213

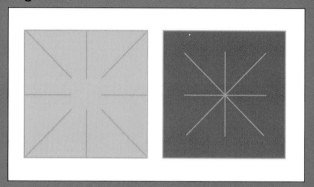

Here you can see the cuts in the paper sheets which allow you to form an eight-pointed star.

Page 214

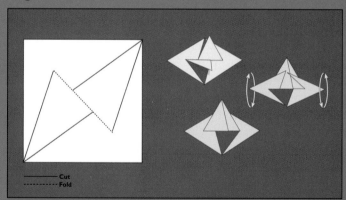

Page 215

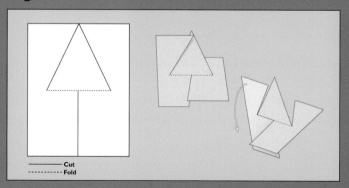

Page 217

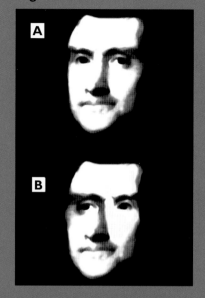

The effect is due to the ambiguity of the face. In fact, we have modified a real unidirectional face (A) by inverting symmetrically the top of the face around a vertical axis. The result (B) is a bidirectional ambiguous face. Our judgment of where a person is fixing his or her gaze is influenced by set, and in this particular case there are two possible sets in just one image.

Page 221

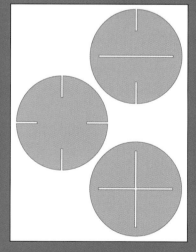

Here is the secret: cut as shown in the example above before you interlock them.

Page 224

Illusory motion is induced by the visual contrasts of the top and its background.

Page 225

We tend to perceive the inset and the surrounding rhombi as two independent fields even though they are on the same plane. The surrounding rhombi are interpreted as a "frame of reference" and tend to be stationary. The visual contrasts of the inset and the surroundings in the picture seem to confuse the motion detector of our visual system.

Page 226

This is a variant of the Ouchi illusion. When you make eye movements while following the picture, the visual contrast of the foreground and background patterns may induce illusory motion at the edges of the central disc. This kind of illusion is thought to arise from retinal motion signals (the motion detector of our visual system). Another interesting observation: the boundaries of the ring which include the Ouchi disc appear to shine slightly, like a neon.

Page 227

The circular set of playing cards with the ace of hearts rotates faster than the circular set with the ace of clubs.

Page 228

Yes, but it is just an illusion induced by the alternating of small light and dark strokes. It is a kind of after-image effect caused by the lateral inhibition of our retina.

Page 229

Yes; the van can contain all the boxes.

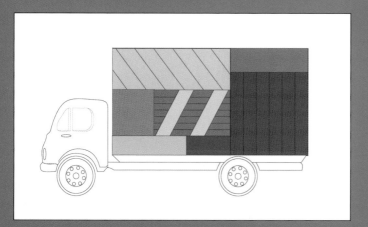

Page 230

It is reversible. It remains a magic square even if you turn it upside-down! And if you look at it from a certain distance, the corners of the small orange squares (containing the numbers) lose their regularity and seem to sharpen.

Page 231

It is no secret, and painters have known for centuries that colors tend to influence each other. Here, two effects are responsible for the apparition of the colors flesh-pink and blue: contrast of color and assimilation of color.

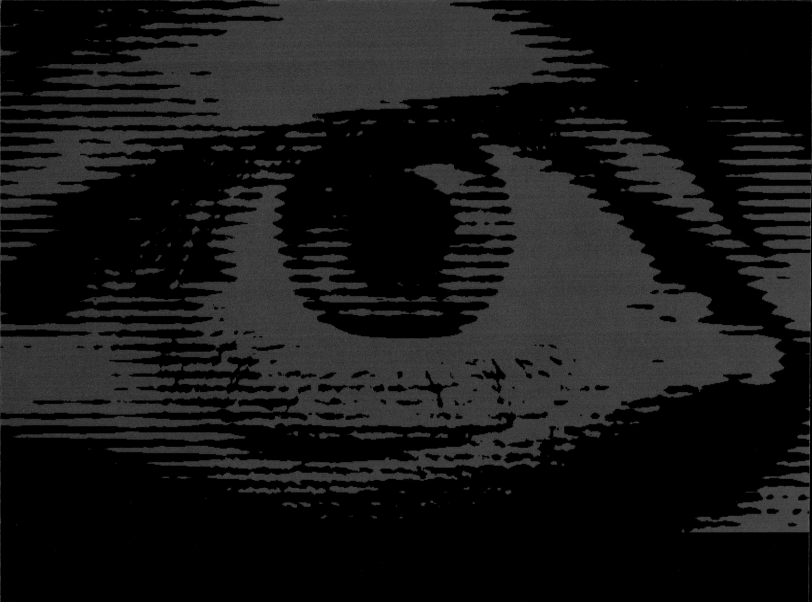

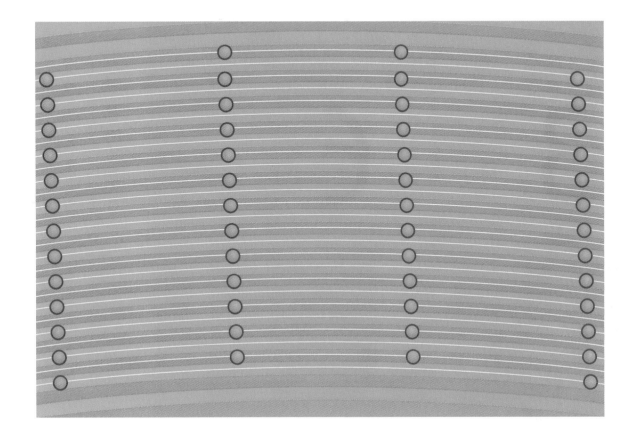

Aligned dots?

It seems incredible, but all the dots are the same shade of pink and the dots that appear clearer are perfectly aligned with those which appear darker. Take a ruler and verify the situation for yourself! These illusions are induced by two factors: contrast of colors and the bended colored lines.

A

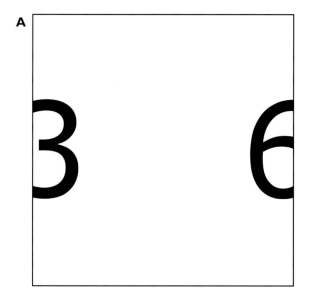

B

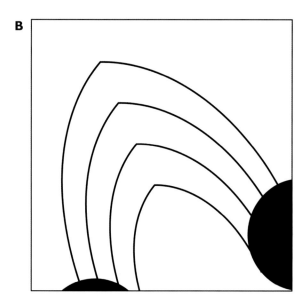

Droodles
What do images A and B represent?

3D Sundial

This picture of a sundial seems confused and flat. Close one eye, and look along the direction indicated by the blue triangle at the bottom of the illustration, leaning the book back as you look. What happens?

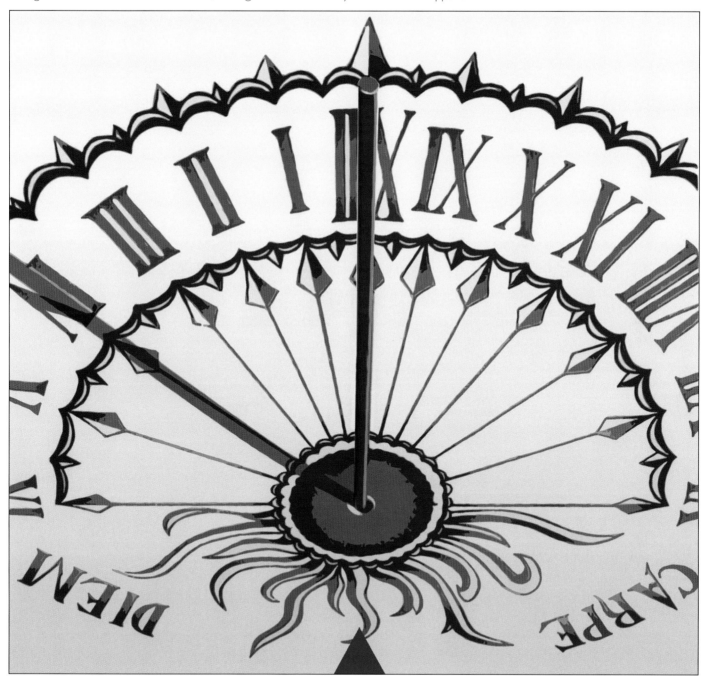

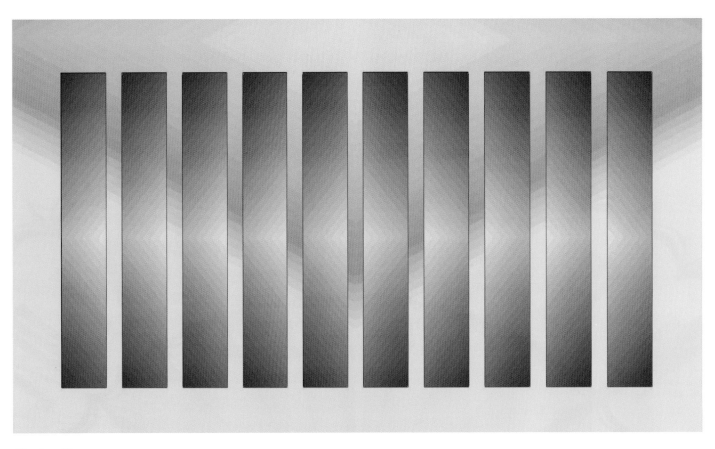

Shade effects
Shade may induce objects, like the parallel slats here, to bulge.

Self-referring word
This image represents a self-referential word (the word "clock" with a clock inside). A self-referential graphic word is a word that encapsulates the thing it represents within itself, like: ei8ht, dOt, lllree, f l rst, para//e/, etc. Can you determine why *semordnilap* is a self-referential word?

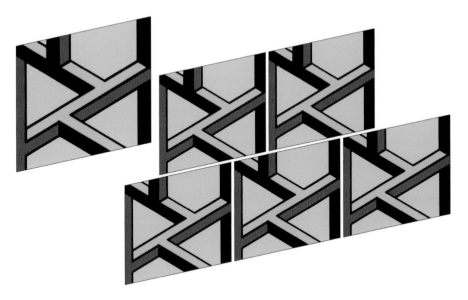

Impossible figure tiles

With the parallelogram tile, it is possible to assemble an impossible structure.

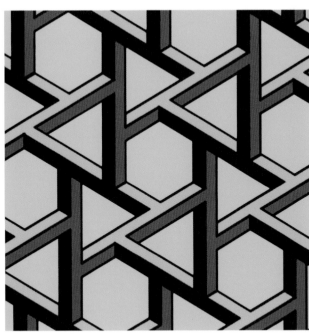

Triangularize it
Using these three "blocks," form the
representation of a pyramid.

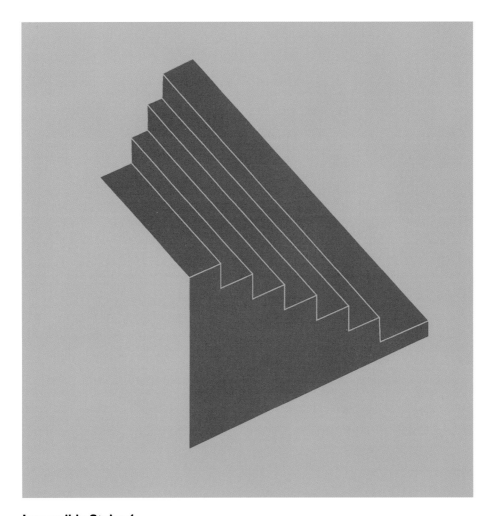

Impossible Stairs 4

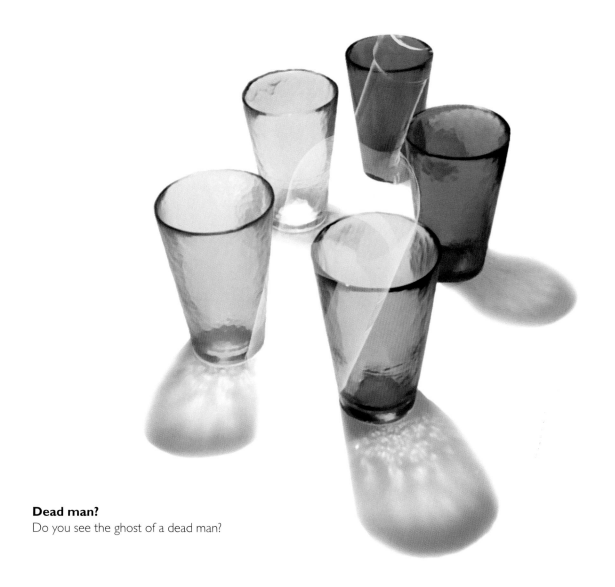

Dead man?
Do you see the ghost of a dead man?

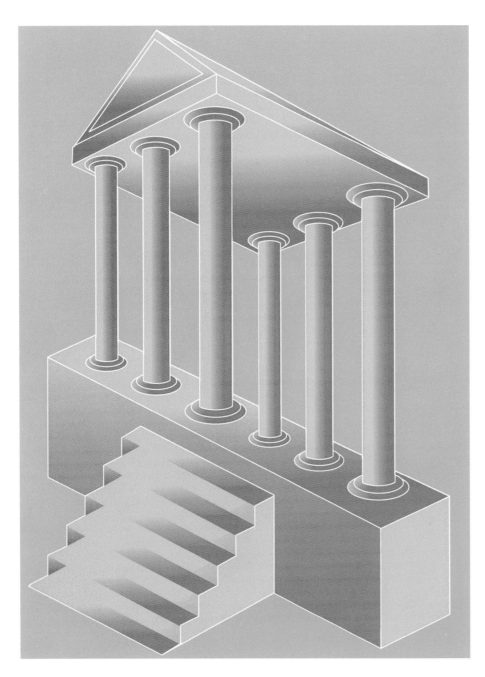

Bidimensional temple

Observe the scene: there are several architectural absurdities!

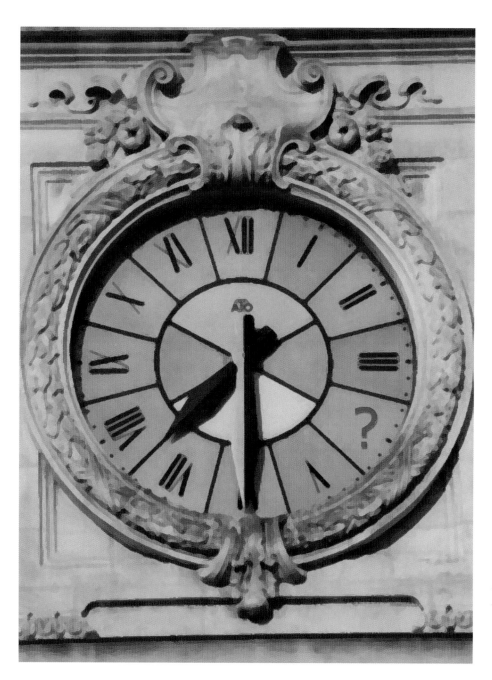

Visual memory test
Trick question: can you remember which
Roman symbols represent four on
most tower clock dials?

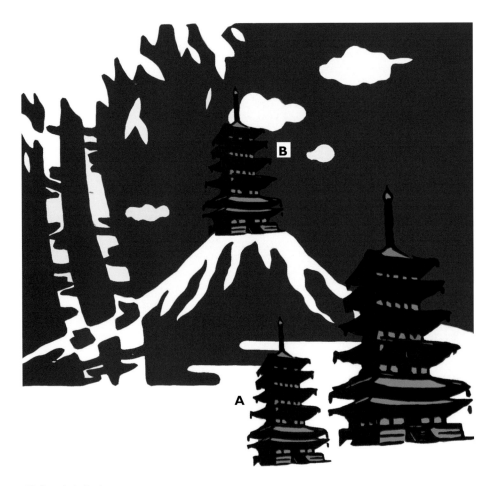

Celestial shrines
Which shrine is taller: A or B?

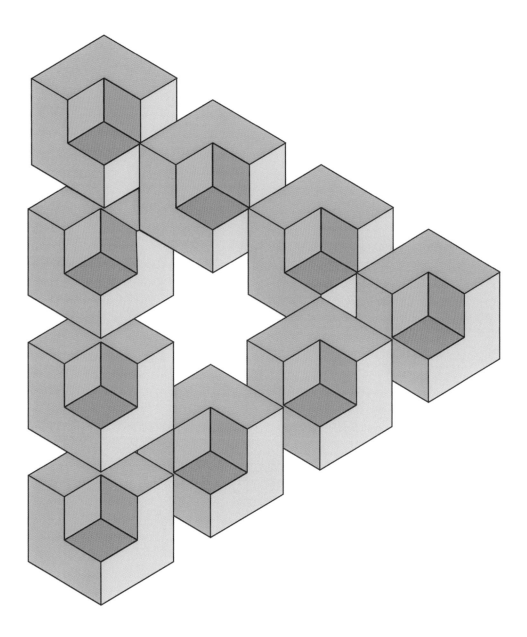

Cubic tribar

In this impossible figure, called a tribar, do you see two sets of cubes
or just one set of cubes with a small cube cut out?

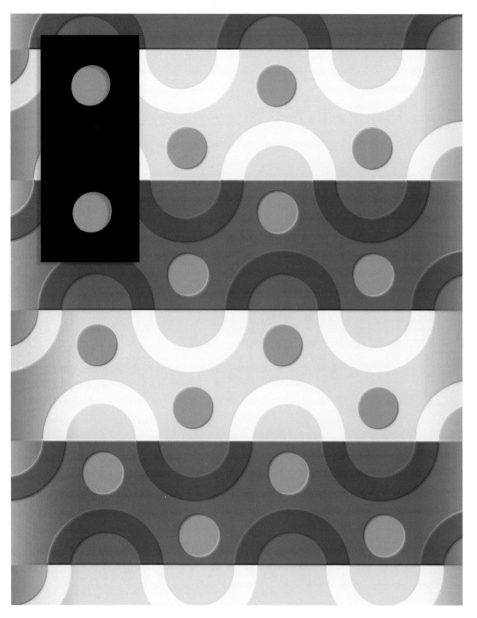

Blues

The blue spots set on the darker background appear lighter than the blue spots on the clearer background. But all the blue spots have identical hues! This compelling visual phenomenon is described as simultaneous lightness contrast.

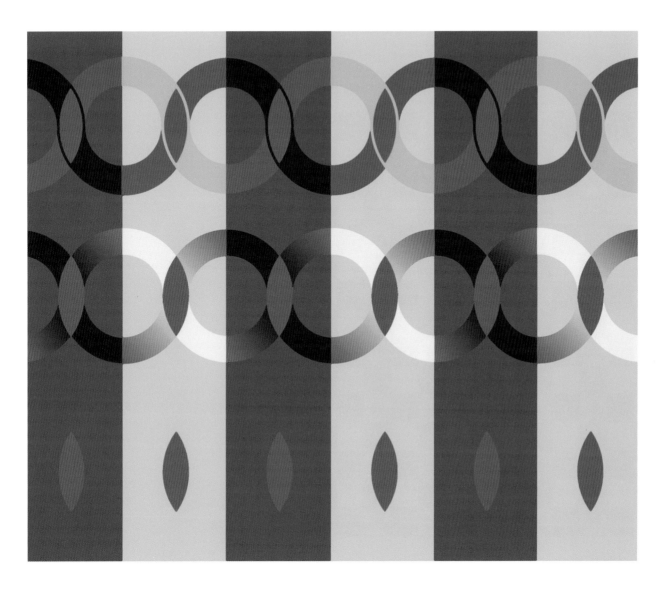

Braids of shade

Three intriguing variants of simultaneous lightness contrast involving lenticular colored shapes (you can see at the bottom of the illustration how the lenticular colored shapes really appear). The two upper examples combine multiple color boundaries and lead to a strong illusion.

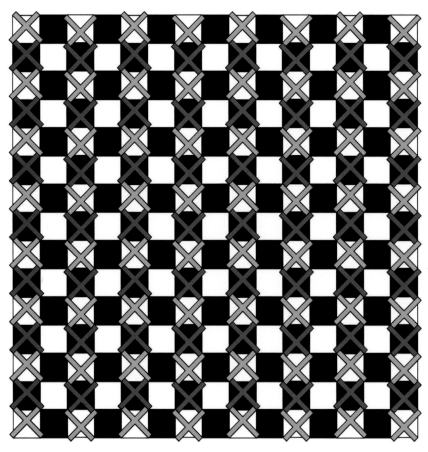

Distorted checkerboard
Alternating cross patterns make the columns of the checkerboard diverge.

Find the hidden shape 1

Can you find the square in the triangle with your naked eye?

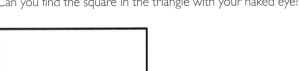

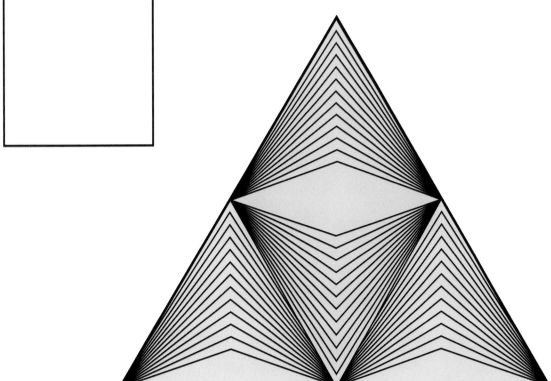

In common

What do the wrought-iron gates have in common?

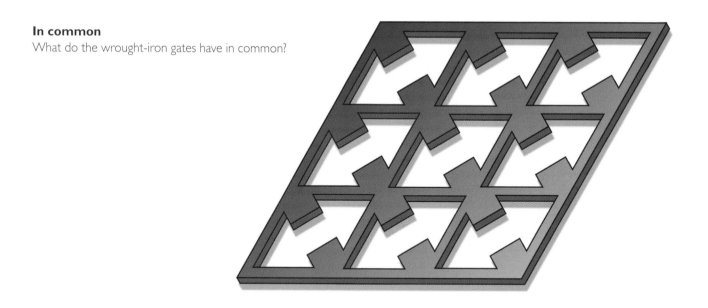

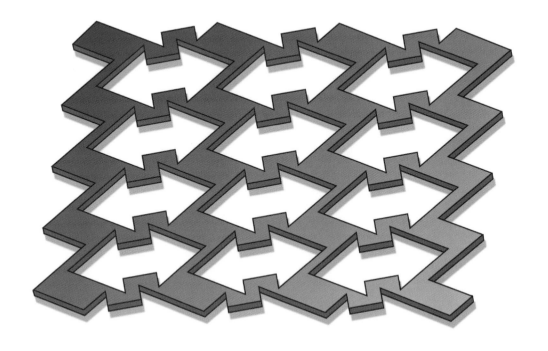

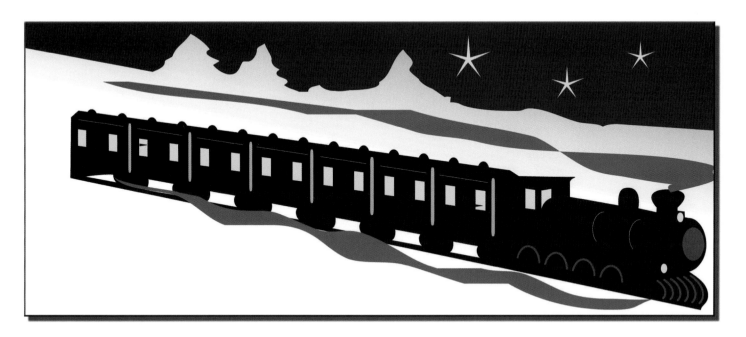

Old Trans-Siberian

Reproduce the card depicting an old Trans-Siberian train and cut it into three pieces. Then rearrange the rectangular card again in order to transform this seven-carriage train into a six-carriage one.

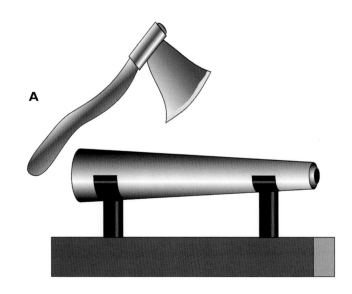

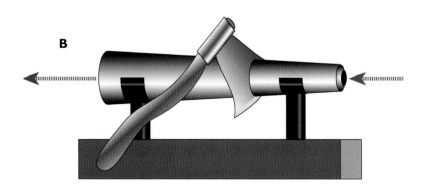

Slashed telescope

The telescope shown in Fig. A is split by an axe into two pieces (Fig. B). Explain why it still works and why it is possible to see through the axe (hint: the axe is not transparent! It is just a question of reflections).

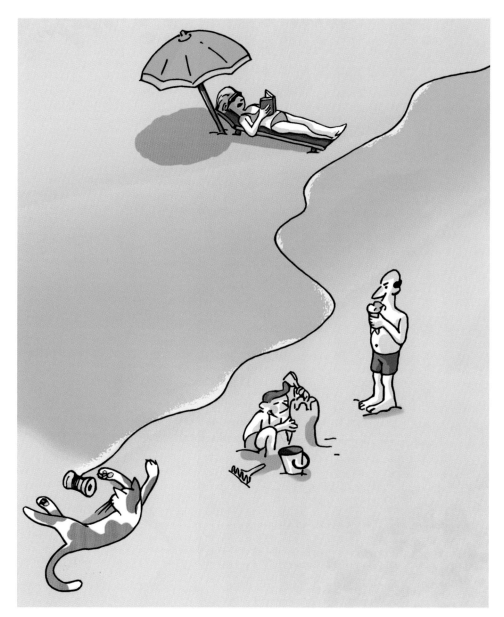

A midsummer day's dream
Just enjoy this picture, which contains this absurdity.

Gallery X Notes

Page 236
The droodle A is a trombone player doing some stretching exercises before a performance. The droodle B is part of a spider's legs while it stands on a mirror.

Page 237
You will soon notice that the upright stick in the center of the sundial (the pointer) rises (and shrinks in height) all by itself.

Page 239
As *semordnilap* is "palindromes" written backwards; it's a self-referential word!

Page 241

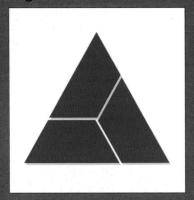

Page 243
It was a joke... 'Dead man' is a little-used British expression for an empty liquor or wine bottle. You will, of course, have noticed a ghostly translucent wine bottle in the picture, but its outline is only determined by the five glasses! The white background within the outline seems slightly yellowish, but in reality, it is uniformly white.

Page 245
On most clock dials you may find the Roman figures IIII for 4, instead of IV. Here is another curiosity about dials. Tell a friend that you are able to guess the position of the hands of any watch featured in a magazine. Then ask him to browse a magazine of his choice and to concentrate on the first advertisement representing a watch he may find. The minute and hour hands will most probably point to 10 past 10. These experiments are based on peculiar traditions and customs which pass unobserved by most people.

Page 246
Our intuition about perspective strongly influences what we see...

Though shrine B appears larger, both shrines are actually the same height. This is a variation of the Ponzo illusion.

Page 247
You may see one or two sets of cubes, or even both, depending on how you look at them. The illusion combines two illusions in one: an impossible figure together with an ambiguous figure.

Page 248
The observation that a color looks darker when set against white than when set against black has puzzled scientists and philosophers for two millennia, yet there is still no consensus as to exactly why it happens. Interesting observations and comments on this subject are provided by scientists Edward Adelson (lightness induction) and Alexander Logvinenko (lightness-shadow invariance).

Page 249
All the lenticular colored shapes are of the same shade, but we see lighter and darker lenticular shapes. We encounter a similar effect in our everyday life: the screen of the television and of the PC aren't black at all, nor can black be created by the electron beams. But when you switch on your television you can see all the colors, black included!

Page 250
All the columns are perfectly parallel and aligned. This illusion is related to the Zöllner illusion.

Page 251

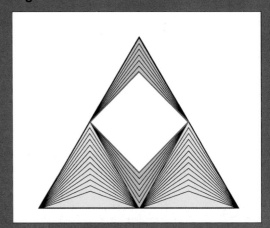

Page 252
Observe the empty spaces... Both gates have the same arrow-shaped empty spaces. When you notice them, you cannot miss them anymore because they become insistent in your visual field.

Page 253

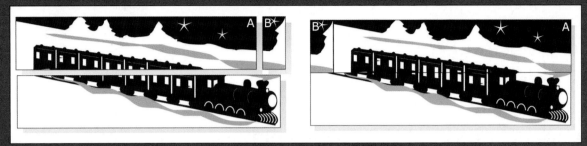

The steam train will lose a wagon depending on the way pieces A and B of the puzzle are reassembled.

Page 254

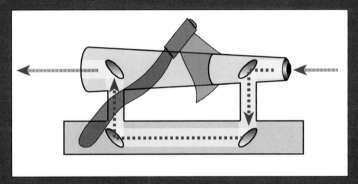

The trick lies in the four mirrors concealed in the telescope's prop.

Gallery XI

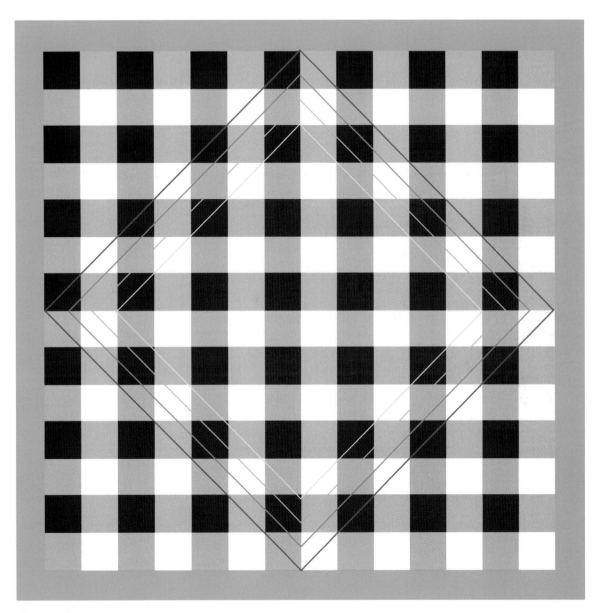

Good vibrations

Are the colors really vibrating? The checkered background induces the color outlines to vibrate slightly. This is a kind of after-image effect and is mainly due to lateral inhibition.

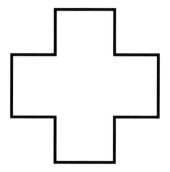

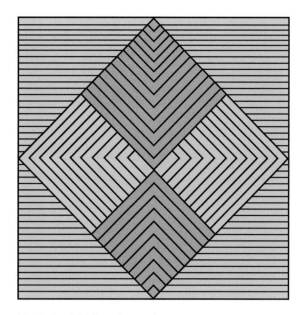

Find the hidden shape 1
Find the cross in the square!

Find the hidden shape 2
Follow your star... Find it in the pattern.

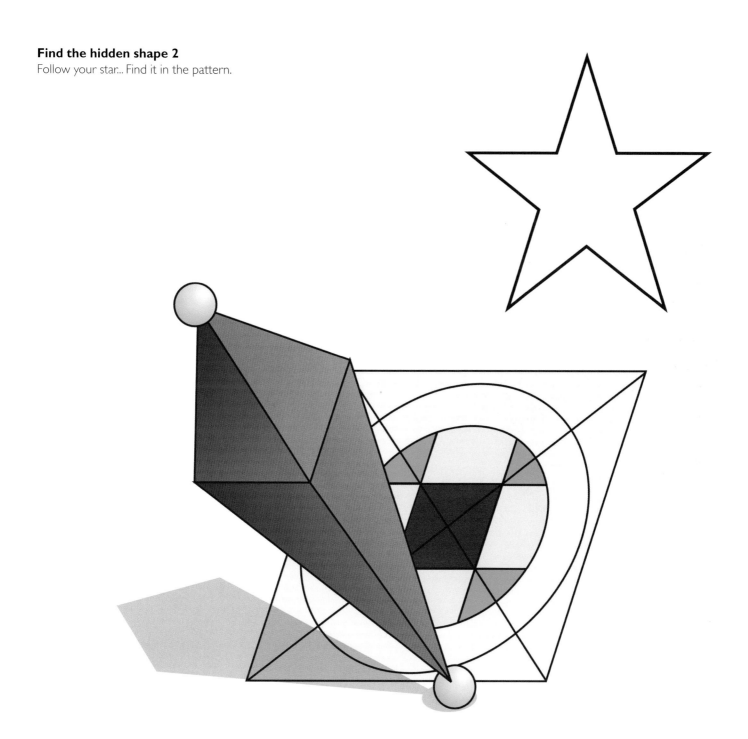

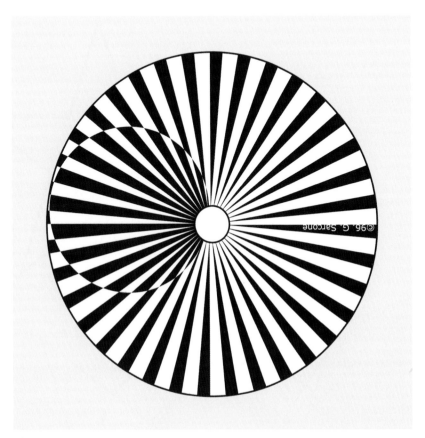

Artificial spectrum top

Reproduce this circular pattern and paste it onto a piece of cardboard, then cut out the disc. Push a short, pointed pencil through its center. You now have a top with magic properties. Spin the top and you'll see subjective colors while it rotates.

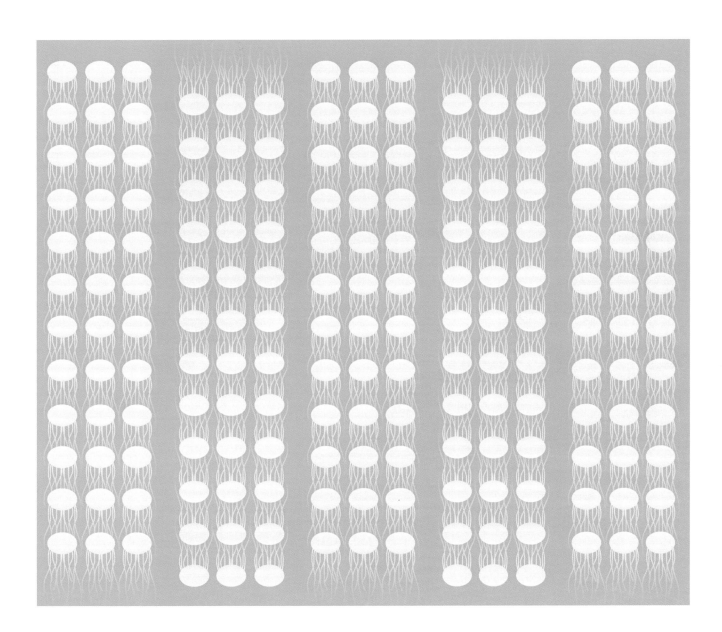

Moving jellyfish

Stare at the image and imagine that the blue is the sea. Concentrate and cast your eyes around the groups of jellyfish and they will start to move in opposite directions.

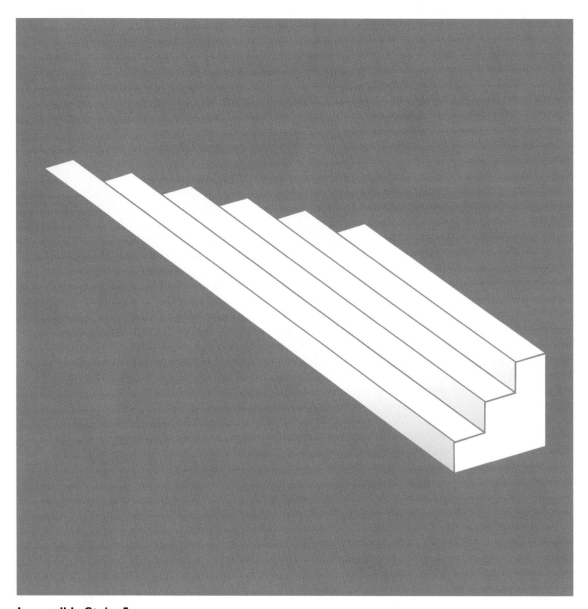

Impossible Stairs 5

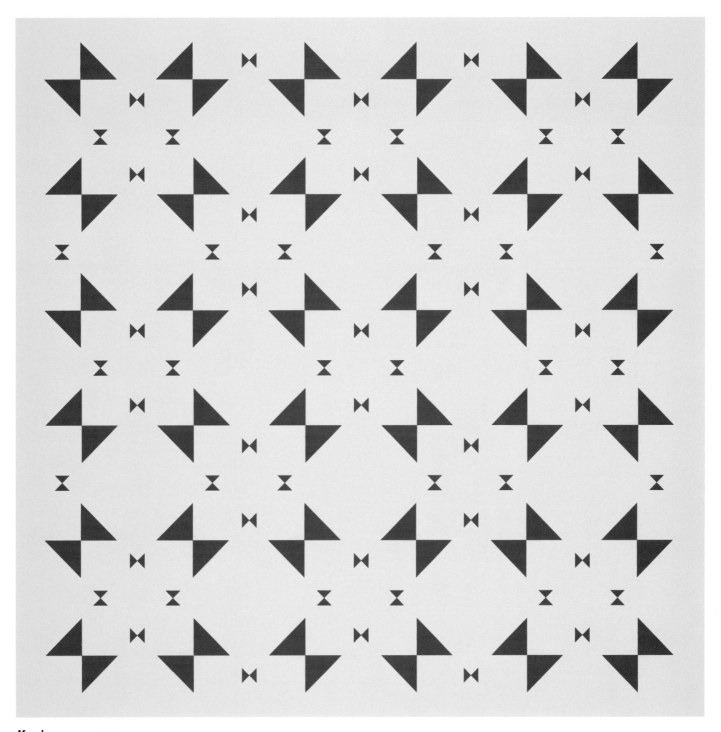

Kanisza squares

How many perfect squares do you perceive?

Running water

Do the blue lines twist up and down like a water flow? Please, turn off the faucets once you've experienced the illusion!

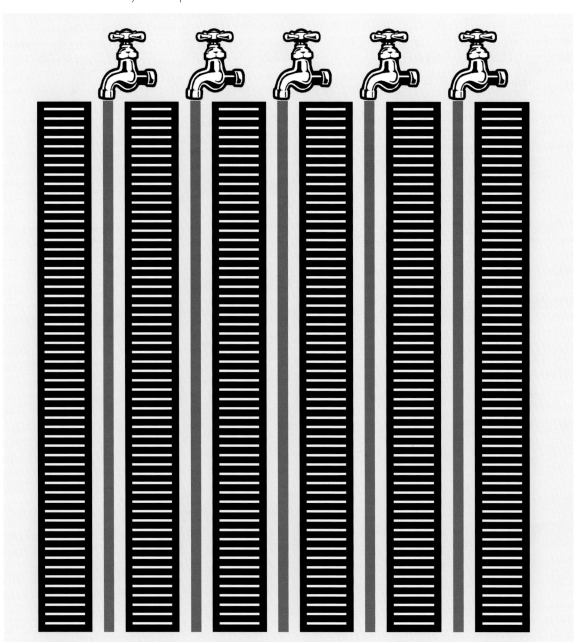

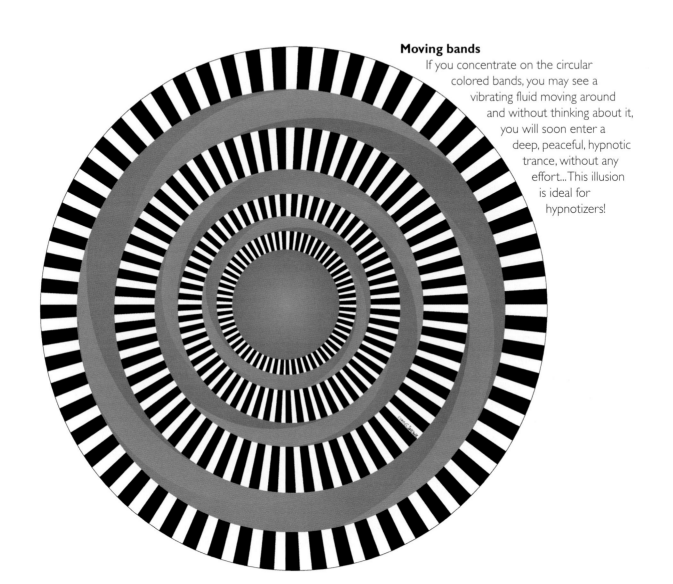

Moving bands
If you concentrate on the circular colored bands, you may see a vibrating fluid moving around and without thinking about it, you will soon enter a deep, peaceful, hypnotic trance, without any effort... This illusion is ideal for hypnotizers!

Gallery XI Notes

Page 260

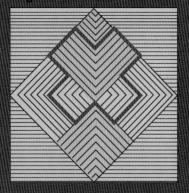

Page 261

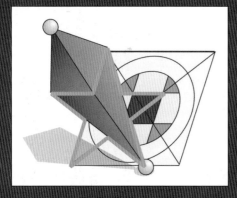

Page 262
The color observed with such rotating discs does not exist. If the disc is rotated in one direction, colors of red to blue may appear. If the disc is rotated in the other direction, the colors appear in the reverse order. Colors obtained with this top are subjective colors or – using a scientific term – pattern-induced flicker colors. The effect observed depends on the intensity of the light source, the speed of rotation and the design and distribution of the black lines. Observation in bright sunshine gives very satisfactory results.
There isn't a complete and certain explanation concerning the observance of subjective colors. Lateral inhibition and the different rates of stimulation for the color receptors in the eye are clearly involved.

Page 263
This illusory motion is related to the central drift illusion. The factor that induces this illusion may be the difference in contrast between the inner and outer areas of the moving objects (jellyfish).

Page 265

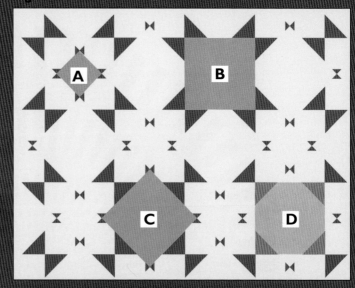

In the picture there are 13 small squares A, 13 squares B, 12 squares C and 12 squares D. In total, there are 50 squares.

Page 266
The illusion is due to lateral inhibition.

Page 267
Another lateral inhibition effect.

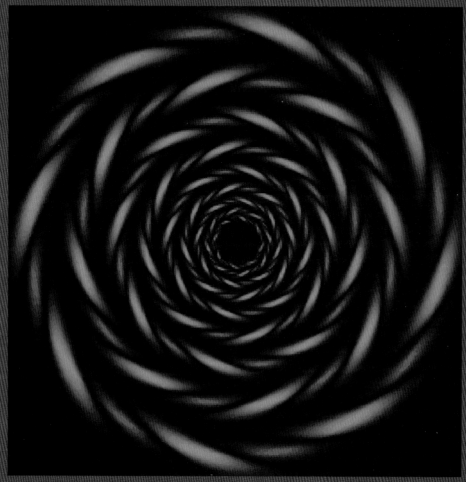

Concentric or not?

At a certain distance, the circles composed of twisted strands of rope of two different colors, may appear confused and diverging. This illusion is sometimes known as the 'twisted cord illusion' and it actually consists of perfectly concentric circles of twisted cords. The visual distortion is produced by combining a regular line pattern (the concentric circles) with misaligned parts (the differently colored strands). Zöllner and the café wall illusions are based on a similar principle, like many other visual effects, in which a sequence of tilted elements causes the eye to perceive phantom twists and deviations.

Glossary

Ambigram
A graphic word or sentence that can be read in more than one way. This can be achieved in several ways: by writing the word so that it can be interpreted in more than one way, or by making it meaningful when turned upside-down.

Ambiguous figues
Open to more than one interpretation. It means that an image as a whole can display different scenes, depending on the interpretation of the viewer.

Blind spot
We cannot see where the optical nerve enters our eye. We don't ever notice it because our eyes constantly make small movements, and above all, our mind just fills in the gap. It just guesses what should be there. The blind spot is actually quite big, as you can see by taking the test on page 139 in this book.

Color contrast and color assimilation
Color contrast refers to the change of hue when colors are perceived in the context of other colors. For instance, colors may look lighter or darker with respect to the background color, or even shift their hues into the direction of the complementary background color. When the areas of color in a pattern are very small, an effect opposite to simultaneous color contrast occurs: colors appear to become more like their neighbor instead of less like them.

Entasis
The slight convex curve used on Greek columns. This curve compensates for the optical illusion that a straight column seems concave.

Hidden images and Camouflage
Camouflage has been used for disguise in the natural world ever since predators developed eyes to track prey. In optical illusions, it is the art of hiding something elegantly in an image. Most often these are landscapes or natural scenes where extra animals or objects are hidden.

Impossible images
Impossible figures can be drawn on paper, but can't exist in real life.

Lateral inhibition
Some photoreceptors of the retina are activated when they detect light, while others are activated in the absence of light. These two types usually encircle each other and are spread throughout the retina creating receptive fields. Often, light can fall onto both light and dark photoreceptors causing the two regions to compete with one another. One part of the receptive field wants to become active while the other part does not. This competitive interaction is called lateral inhibition. Because of this antagonistic nature of receptive fields, perceptual illusions, such as the Herman grid illusion, can occur when we look at certain patterns.

Pareidolia
A kind of illusion or misperception where something meaningless is considered meaningful. For example, recognizing a giraffe in a cloud.

Procrypsis
The ability to blend into the background. This environmental camouflage is most often seen with insects and many animals. Just think of walking sticks and those weird bugs that look like leaves.

Upside-down images
An upside-down or topsy turvy image is an image showing something meaningful when turned around. That can be one thing, or something completely different.

Recent works by the same authors
Almanach du Mathématicien en Herbe, Sarcone & Wäber, Edition Archimède, Paris, 2002.
Matemagica, Sarcone & Wäber, La Meridiana Editore, Italy, 2005.

Some resourceful and richly illustrated books
Visual Games, Franco Agostini, 1980 (unique!).
Can You Believe Your Eyes?, J. Block & H. Yuker, Mazel Publisher, 1992.
The Playful Eye, Mel Gooding, Redstone Press, 1999.
Adventures with Impossible Objects, Bruno Ernst, Evergreen Editor, 2002.

Original and interesting sites on optical illusions
http://www.archimedes-lab.org/index_optical.html
  (Archimedes Lab's perceptual illusion site)
http://www.michaelbach.de/ot/ (optical illusions by a specialist)
http://www.ritsumei.ac.jp/~akitaoka/index-e.html
  (A. Kitaoka's optical illusion site)
http://members.lycos.co.uk/brisray/optill/vision3.htm
  (Perceptual Science Group, MIT)
http://web.mit.edu/persci/people/adelson/illusions_demos.html
  (E. Adelson's optical illusion site)
http://members.lycos.nl/amazingart/E/index.html (amazing art site)
http://www.planetperplex.com/en/optical_illusions.html
  (perplexing illusions)

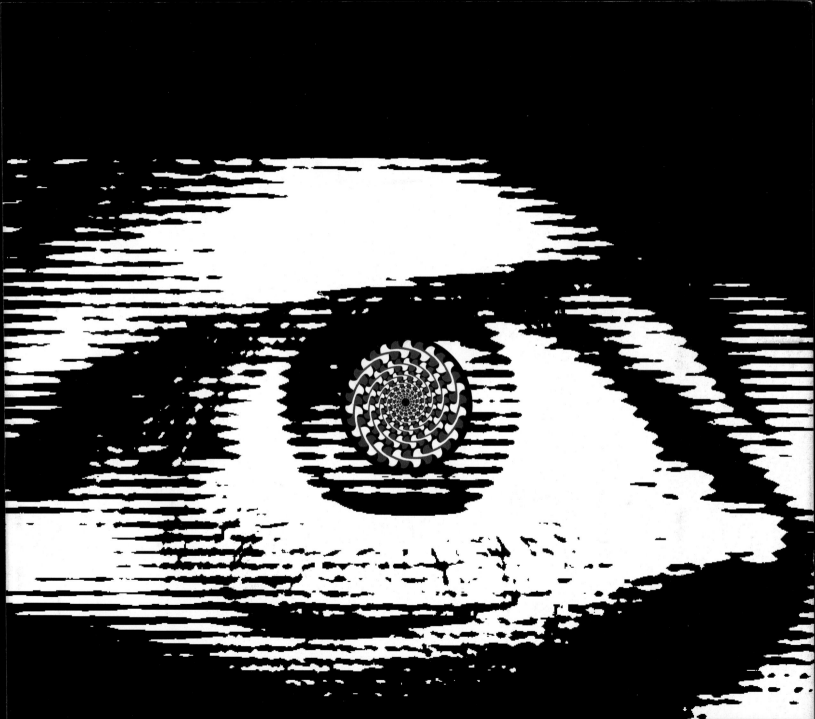

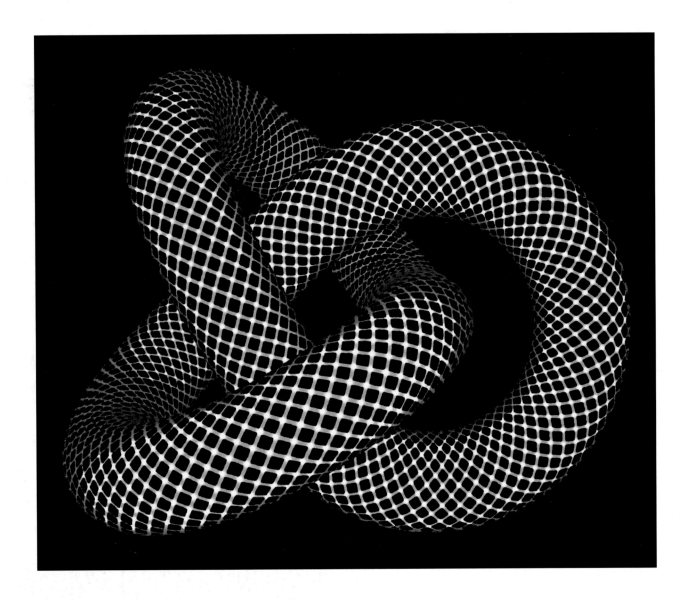

Picture credits

The authors would like to acknowledge the following sources. Any oversights, omissions, or corrections will be updated in future editions of this work.

Pages 41, 108: Apparent rotations and Peripheral drift illusion based on research by J. Flaubert and A. Herbert.

Page 51: Peculiar cubic network based on Escher cubic space division illusion.

Page 101: Simultaneous brightness contrast based on Adelson checker-shadow illusion.

Page 102: Ghost triangle based on Kanisza triangle illusion.

Page 226: Floating disc inspired by a design of Hajime Ouchi.

Page 249: Braids of shade inspired by a design of E. Adelson (criss-cross illusion).